Quiknotes

*Christian
History*

Here are some other useful books
in the *Quiknotes* series.
Add them to your library of
quick-reference books today

QUIKNOTES: THE BOOKS OF THE BIBLE
QUIKNOTES: THE BOOKS OF THE NEW TESTAMENT
QUIKNOTES: THE BOOKS OF THE OLD TESTAMENT
QUIKNOTES: THE ORIGIN OF THE BIBLE
QUIKNOTES: ENGLISH BIBLE VERSIONS
QUIKNOTES: DEVOTIONAL CLASSICS
QUIKNOTES: GREAT WOMEN OF FAITH

Quiknotes™
CHRISTIAN
HISTORY

by Paul R. Waibel

Tyndale House Publishers, Inc.
WHEATON, ILLINOIS

Visit Tyndale's exciting Web site at www.tyndale.com

[Library of Congress Cataloging-in-Publication Data]

Waibel, Paul R.
  Christian history / by Paul R. Waibel.
    p. cm.—(Quiknotes)
  Includes bibliographical references and index.
  ISBN 0-8423-3331-2 (sc)
  I. Church history.   I. Title.   II. Quiknotes (Wheaton, Ill.)
BR150.W35 2000
270—dc21   00-037782

Printed in the United States of America

09 08 07 06 05 04 03 02 01 00
10 9   8   7   6   5   4   3   2   1

CONTENTS

PREFACE

Quiknotes: Christian History is intended to meet the need for a concise yet comprehensive survey of the significant themes of church history during the past two millennia. It is intended for the layperson or student who desires a brief introduction to church history.

The book is "user friendly" in several ways. The writing is clear and, hopefully, engaging enough to keep the reader turning the page. The overall approach is chronological and follows the normal outline of history from the Roman Empire through the Middle Ages, Reformation, Enlightenment, to the twentieth century. Attention is given to the interaction between major events in both secular and church history. At the beginning of each chapter, a paragraph entitled "The Big Picture" has been included to give readers a quick summary of the events and themes that will be covered in that chapter. This is followed by a short list of "Key Events." At the end of each chapter a more extensive timeline has been provided. Several of the chapters include tables or lists to clarify specific events or to provide an overview of certain themes. A bibliography of suggested books has also been included for those who wish to read further on various topics mentioned in this book.

Quiknotes: Christian History is based upon secondary sources and an understanding of history derived from more than twenty years of teaching history in Christian colleges. To some extent this book is a product of what I have learned from those many years of interacting with students and colleagues inside and outside the classroom. Certainly a major debt of gratitude is owed to the folks at Tyndale House for granting me the opportunity to write this volume for the *Quiknotes* series and to the editorial staff, the folks in design and others whose expertise was able to transform my manuscript pages into a book. Finally, a deep debt of gratitude is owed to my student assistant, Miss Sarah Pasarilla, who helped put the index together; to my wife, Darlene, who read each chapter and made helpful suggestions for improvement; and to my two daughters, Elizabeth Joy and Natalie Grace, who gave me their patience and cheerful support. I offer this book with the hope that the reader will find it informative and enjoyable.

Paul R. Waibel

INTRODUCTION

The history of the church over the past two millennia has both shaped and been shaped by the secular culture. It was the teachings of the church that made Western civilization distinct from other civilizations. During the fourth century, the pilgrim church of the New Testament, a church that transformed the Roman world while suffering persecution, gave way to an imperial church. During the fourth through the tenth centuries, Judeo-Christianity blended with classical humanism and the Germanic traditions to produce Christendom.

During the period of medieval Christendom, Christianity was the glue in the medieval synthesis. By reconciling faith and reason, the church made peace with humanistic philosophy. But the acceptance of humanistic philosophy (e.g., Aristotle and Plato) led to doctrinal corruption. Until the sixteenth century the church experienced revival through the founding of new monastic orders. Such revivals were possible because the new orders of monks and friars did not challenge the authority of the papacy. That changed with the appearance of Martin Luther in 1517.

The sixteenth-century Protestant Reformation arose out of the conviction that the corruption in the church was due to corrupt doctrine. The solution offered was a return to the authority of the Bible. By reasserting the biblical doctrine of salvation by grace through faith, the Protestant Reformers called into question the necessity of the whole medieval church as then constituted. The Reformation was made possible in part by the emergence of nation-states and weakening of feudalism. So as not to alarm the new monarchs who saw in the Reformation the opportunity for creating national churches, the mainline Reformers endorsed territorial churches and rejected the idea of a gathered out, or believers church. Hence, the radical reformers (e.g., Anabaptists) suffered persecution from both Roman Catholic and Protestant leaders.

Once the unity of Christendom had been broken, the new Protestant faiths spent the seventeenth century defining their doctrinal positions. This century of dead orthodoxy, as it is often called, left the established churches ill-prepared for the secularization of Western civilization that grew out of the eighteenth-century Enlightenment. However, with the secularism of the Enlightenment came religious tolerance. This opened the door for the revival known as the Great Awakening in America, Evangelicalism in England, Pietism on the continent, and Quietism in the Catholic church.

Out of German Pietism came the birth of the modern Protestant foreign mission movement, begun by the Moravians. The nineteenth century became the great century of Protestant foreign missions, especially as European imperialism began to open doors previously closed to such activity. Not only missions, but a concern for social reform characterized the revivals of the nineteenth century. Evangelical Christians struggled in the forefront of the movements to end slavery and mitigate the evils of the Industrial Revolution.

By the beginning of the twentieth century, Western civilization dominated the world. Many Christians equated the westernization of the world with its Christianization, believing that this would hasten the return of Jesus Christ. Such optimism suffered a devastating blow from the coming of World War I and the subsequent end of Western domination in the world.

World War I was a catalyst for fundamental changes that had

been occurring in Western thought since the last half of the nineteenth century. By the 1920s, Western intellectuals had abandoned the basic values, or tenets, of Western civilization. The belief in the value of the individual as a reasoning creature was abandoned. Instead, people living in the modern era began to see themselves as irrational animals, adrift in a world of random chaos. Those theologies that tried to reconcile biblical Christianity with the new assumptions (e.g., modernism, liberalism, and neo-orthodoxy) failed to meet the deep-felt needs of individuals suffering in the Great Depression and in the Second World War.

Those who defended the doctrines of the early church as reaffirmed by the Reformation became known as fundamentalists. Fundamentalism, more a state of mind than a doctrinal position, gave way to a new evangelical revival after World War II. This new evangelicalism was characterized by diversity. It included scholarly responses to the new postmodern secular intellectualism, the evangelism of Billy Graham, and charismatic revival. By the end of the twentieth century, evangelicalism in the West appeared mired in materialism, while revival swept through the non-Western societies of Latin America, Africa, and Asia.

In the chapters that follow, each of these topics and themes will be explored more fully, giving the reader a general grasp of the story of Christianity. We will see how it has affected and been affected by the world in which it has taken shape over the past two millennia.

CHAPTER 1

In the Beginning: The Early Church to A.D. 325

THE BIG PICTURE

The first period of church history parallels the history of the Roman Empire. From the time the Christian church was first founded at Pentecost until the Jerusalem Council (49 or 50) or the Jewish revolt and destruction of the temple (66–70), the church existed primarily within Judaism. The Jerusalem Council opened the church to Gentiles, defining salvation as coming by grace through faith in the risen Lord Jesus Christ, rather than by adherence to the laws of Moses. The apostle Paul developed a theology for the new universal church. The church was a "pilgrim church" until the emperor Constantine legalized Christianity in 312 and the Council of Nicaea, meeting under imperial authority, defined what it meant to be an orthodox Christian. Because of this pilgrim status, the Christians in this era suffered persecution first from the Jewish establishment and then from the Roman state. After 325, the church became an "established church," enjoying the favor of the state, especially after 381, when the emperor Theodosius I made Christianity the only legal religion in the Roman Empire.

KEY EVENTS

c. 30   The coming of the Holy Spirit at Pentecost marks the beginning of the Christian church.

c. 49/50   At the Jerusalem Council the Christian church begins to separate itself from Judaism and becomes a universal church accessible to everyone.

313   The emperor Constantine issues the Edict of Milan, granting tolerance to Christians and thus ending persecution of Christians in the Roman Empire.

325   Meeting under imperial authority, the Council of Nicaea defines orthodox belief, thus ending the era of the "pilgrim church" and inaugurating the era of the "established church."

On Passover Eve in the year A.D. 30, when Pontius Pilate was procurator (actually prefect, or governor) of Judea, Jesus was arrested. Taken first before a Jewish court, Jesus was charged with sedition and turned over to Pilate. Though Pilate believed Jesus innocent of the charge, for political reasons he gave in to the wishes of the Jewish authorities and condemned Jesus to death by crucifixion. In accordance with Pilate's judgment, Jesus was executed by Roman soldiers in Jerusalem at a site known as Golgotha, or Calvary. No doubt, those who condemned Jesus thought his death would be the end of the matter. But they were wrong. What occurred in Jerusalem on that Passover was not an accident of history, but the fulfillment of Old Testament prophecy.

Three days after Jesus' death, the word spread throughout Jerusalem that Jesus was not dead, that he had been raised from the dead, and that he had appeared to his disciples. The Jewish authorities tried to combat the news of Jesus' resurrection with the rumor that his disciples had stolen his body. But they never questioned the fact that the tomb was empty or produced a body. Indeed, no authority since has ever questioned the fact that on that first Easter morning, the tomb was empty.

During the forty days following his resurrection, Jesus appeared to his disciples on several occasions, not as a disembodied spirit but physically. He ate with them, and, most importantly, he explained to them the meaning of his suffering and death. He promised them that they would receive power with the coming of the Holy Spirit, after which, they were to proclaim the good news of his life, death, and resurrection in "Jerusalem, and in all Judea and Samaria, and to the ends of the earth" (Acts 1:8). Thus Jesus was the foundation upon which the Holy Spirit would found the church.

Obedient to their risen Lord's command, the disciples remained in Jerusalem during the seven weeks following Passover. Then on the day of Pentecost (a Jewish festival celebrated fifty days after the beginning of Passover), the promised Holy Spirit descended upon the assembled disciples with signs of divine power. The commotion was such that a crowd began to gather—Jews from throughout the Roman Empire were in Jerusalem for the festival. Luke records in the book of Acts that these "God-fearing Jews" were "amazed and perplexed" to hear the disciples speaking in their own languages. Since the disciples were Galileans, some disbelieved their ears and said that the men were simply drunk. Peter responded to the charge, preaching the first evangelistic sermon of the church. In doing so, he clearly set forth the mission of the church from Pentecost to the present: that under the inspiration of the Holy Spirit, Christians are to proclaim the Good News (gospel) of salvation by grace through faith in the risen Lord Jesus Christ to all who would hear and believe. In response to Peter's message, some three thousand listeners accepted his message and were baptized.

THE CHURCH AMONG THE JEWS

The coming of the Holy Spirit at Pentecost is almost universally understood to be the beginning of the church. The Jews of the Diaspora (those scattered throughout the empire) who were present and who accepted the gospel, soon returned to their homes throughout the Roman Empire, testifying to what had happened to them in Jerusalem. In Jerusalem itself, the disciples—at least Peter and John—began to preach the gospel, accompanied by miraculous signs. Soon there were at least five thousand believers in Jerusalem (Acts 4:4).

Despite the conversion of Jews from other regions of the

Roman Empire at Pentecost, however, the early church still existed primarily within Judaism. Jewish Christians assembled in private homes or in the synagogues until prohibited from doing so around the end of the first century. It was not until the middle of the third century that the first church buildings began to appear. Christians met on Sunday, the first day of the week, since that is the day Jesus was raised from the dead. There were apparently two services. One took place in the morning and consisted of Scripture reading, a message by one of the elders, prayer, and singing. A second service in the evening included a shared meal, or "love feast," prior to the celebration of Communion (established by Jesus the night he was betrayed) by those who had been baptized. Faith in Jesus Christ was the only requirement for baptism during those early years.

The organization of the early church was very simple. All believers were considered priests in their own right, with direct access to God through Jesus Christ. In a sense, this approximated the organization of the church as the body of Christ—a spiritual union of all true believers (past, present, and future) united by the Holy Spirit—with Jesus Christ as the head. In terms of the visible, human institution of the church, however, these Jewish converts modeled its structure after that of the synagogue.

Jesus Christ left no definite organizational structure for this earthly, temporal manifestation of the church. He left behind apostles (most of whom had been Jesus' disciples while he was here on earth) who, acting under the inspiration of the Holy Spirit, appointed additional officers as the need arose. Soon there were elders (or *presbyters*), who formed a collective leadership for a local congregation. They were assisted by deacons and deaconesses, who performed a variety of practical, day-to-day functions, such as the distribution of charity. All were democratically elected by, and from, the individual group of believers, or local congregation.

So long as they were alive, the apostles exercised leadership over the fledgling church. James, the brother of Jesus (although himself not an apostle), together with Peter exercised leadership in the church at Jerusalem—to which all believers looked for guidance. After each of his missionary journeys, Paul reported back to the church in Jerusalem. Clearly, Peter was the dominant figure in the early church. It was Peter who preached the first sermon at Pentecost, and it was he who first took the gospel to the Gentiles when he preached to the household of Cornelius (Acts 10:34-43). The leadership role of the apostles and the importance of the Jerusalem church is very evident in the Jerusalem Council (A.D. 49 or 50), the first, and perhaps most important, council in church history.

The Jerusalem Council sought to clarify the relationship between the church, its Christ-given commission to carry the gospel to all people, and the cultural environment in which the church was developing. The temporal church (the church as it exists on earth) is a human institution (albeit inspired and guided by the Holy Spirit) that exists in a historical moment. It cannot escape the culture in which it exists. For early Christians, this confronted them with the question of whether or not the new Christian church would remain a sect within Judaism.

As the church began growing among the Gentiles, the question arose as to whether or not the new converts had to observe the Jewish ceremonial laws (e.g., circumcision). If the church existed within Judaism, the Gentile converts would have had to observe the laws of Moses in order to be saved. This question existed for some time. Peter, for example, resisted sharing the gospel with Gentiles until the Lord showed him in a vision that nothing God made clean was to be called unclean (Acts 10:15). Unless settled, the issue threatened to separate Jewish and Gentile Christians, hindering the church's efforts to fulfill its great commission. This crisis came to a head when a delegation from Jerusalem, "zealots for the law," visited the largely Gentile church in Antioch.

The visitors from Jerusalem insisted that the Gentile converts be circumcised and conform to the laws of Moses. Similar visits were made to other churches founded by Paul and Barnabas. Paul, who was with Barnabas in Antioch at the time, recognized the danger of this false gospel in his letter to the Galatians. So Paul and Barnabas joined a delegation from the church in Antioch and journeyed to Jerusalem to seek guidance.

In Jerusalem, the matter was placed before the leaders of the church and debated. Peter reminded those present of what the Lord had revealed to him. He was followed by Paul and Barnabas, who witnessed to God's work among the Gentiles through their ministry. Finally, James rose and, appealing to the authority of Scripture (Amos 9:11-12), voiced the decision of the Jerusalem leaders "that [they] should not make it difficult for the Gentiles who are turning to God" (Acts 15:19). Salvation was to be by faith alone, not works. With this decision, the church liberated itself from its Jewish cultural roots. To become a Christian, one need not become a Jew or any other nationality.

The Jerusalem Council did not fully end the Jewish phase of church history. The church was freed from the danger of remaining a minor sect within the Jewish faith, yet Jerusalem remained its important center. Increasingly, however, Antioch began to play a leading role in the church, serving as the home base for Paul's ministry. From Antioch, Paul set out on his journeys, carrying the gospel to the Gentiles in Cyprus, Galatia, Macedonia, Greece, and Asia. Some believe that Paul may have even preached in Spain. In his letters to the churches he helped found, Paul developed a theology for the new, universal church. These letters make up a major portion of the New Testament.

Paul was formerly known as Saul of Tarsus. He had been a devoted Pharisee and a zealous persecutor of the first Christians. On a mission to Damascus, however, the risen Lord Jesus appeared to him, and Paul repented, devoting his life to a gospel of sacrificial love. He preached that Jesus Christ, the perfect God-man, gave his life to redeem the lost. Sinners need only accept on faith what Christ has done on their behalf. Once in a personal relationship with Christ, the Christian's conduct is governed by the law of love. Thus the moral issues that so dominated the life of the church during its Jewish phase were answered. The law was to be written on the heart of the believer.

Peter's ministry after the Jerusalem Council is not documented. The New Testament is silent on his post-council ministry. According to Roman Catholic tradition, Peter founded the church in Rome and served as its first bishop for some twenty-five years, but there is no historical evidence for that tradition. Most scholars agree, however, that Peter was martyred, along with Paul, in A.D. 64 during Nero's persecution in Rome. According to tradition, Peter was crucified upside down. Paul was almost certainly put to death by the sword, a courtesy accorded condemned Roman citizens under Roman law. James, the brother of Jesus, traditionally the first bishop of the Jerusalem church, was martyred in Jerusalem in A.D. 63 at the instigation of the high priest Ananus. The apostle John, the other major apostolic leader of the early church, was exiled to the island of Patmos during the reign of Domitian. After Domitian's death in A.D. 96, John returned to Ephesus, where he died a natural death.

The passing of the apostles is one of the events that marks the close of the Jewish phase of church history. Another is the revolt of the Jews in A.D. 66 and the subsequent fall of Jerusalem to Titus in A.D. 70. Christians in Jerusalem did not support the Jewish revolt. Many left the city to seek refuge in Pella, a city across the Jordan River. The fall of Jerusalem and destruction of the temple accelerated the separation of the Christian church from Judaism. Even in theology, discussions revolving around the moral law were being displaced by increased contact with Hellenistic philosophy. Paul dealt with the challenge of Greek philosophy in his letter to the Christians in Colosse. The challenges of the Jewish cultural environment were replaced with the challenges of a new Greco-Roman cultural environment, as the church became largely Gentile. This opened the Roman phase of its history.

THE CHURCH IN THE ROMAN EMPIRE
. . . .

As the church became independent of Judaism, it found in the Roman Empire a very favorable environment for growth. The period from the founding of the empire by Augustus (27 B.C.–A.D. 14)[1] to the end of the reign of Marcus Aurelius (A.D. 161–180) is known in history as the *Pax Romana,* or "Roman Peace." It was roughly two hundred years during which the Western world was united under one government, one culture (Greco-Roman, or classical), one common language (*Koiné* Greek), and one law. From Britain to North Africa, from Spain to Mesopotamia, merchants could travel on paved roads between a network of cities—the Roman Empire was an urban empire.

Classical culture prevailed in the cities. Even their physical appearance, no matter where they were located in the empire, had in common a certain *Romanitas,* or Roman look. Each had public baths, theaters, temples, statuaries, and other public buildings constructed in a characteristically Roman style. Beneath the surface of an urban cultural unity, however, Rome ruled a multicultural world.

The Roman concept of a rule of law, symbolized in the initials SPQR (The Senate and People of Rome), enabled the Romans to construct the world's only universal state. Christians enjoyed the protection of Roman law, so long as they were regarded as a Jewish sect. Paul, a Roman citizen, enjoyed special protection from the arbitrary will of local officials while on his missionary travels. What the Roman government would not tolerate was anything that threatened to disturb the peace or unity of the empire.

Historians of the period note that the ancient world was experiencing a spiritual crisis during the Roman Empire, especially after the second century A.D. Forced unity meant the loss of local independence. The old Greco-Roman religions drawn from Greek mythology could not satisfy the spiritual longing of those who felt their age was increasingly bankrupt, both morally and spiritually. Many turned to the mystery religions that became popular during the empire. The mystery religions originated in the East, including the cults of Cybele (Asia Minor), Isis

---

[1] Dates for Roman emperors and popes are dates of their reigns. All other dates are birth and death dates.

8

(Egypt), Mithras (Persia), and Emesa, the Unconquerable Sun (Syria), whose birthday was celebrated on December 25.

The mystery religions were secret societies with elaborate initiatory rites. Most featured some god who had died and was resurrected, thus a savior-god. Initiation into one of the mystery religions often included some form of baptism. Initiates into the cult of Cybele, for example, were baptized in a shower of blood as a bull was slaughtered above them. The popularity of the mystery religions evidenced the spiritual bankruptcy of Roman civilization. Participation in them diverted attention momentarily, but they could not satisfy the longing for meaning any more than the gods of Greco-Roman mythology.

The mystery religions had certain things in common with Christianity, but there were profound differences. Jesus was not a myth. He actually lived. He was a historic figure. Most importantly, Jesus was the Son of God who, out of love, had entered history to suffer and die for the sins of humanity. This was a message that could answer the deepest spiritual needs of people then, and today. Finally, Christianity was exclusive. Unlike the pagan religions, it would tolerate no other gods. It was this exclusiveness that brought Christians into conflict with the Roman state.

The Romans were religiously tolerant. The people of the empire were free to worship whatever gods they chose, so long as they acknowledged the sovereignty of the state as embodied in the emperor. Thus Christians, with their claim that Jesus Christ was Lord over all, appeared to be disloyal subjects who were creating a state within a state. This, Rome would not tolerate.

There were other reasons why Romans persecuted Christians. Christians were thought to be atheists, for they did not worship any visible image. A misunderstanding of Christian practices such as Communion (the "love feast") led to charges of incest, cannibalism, and immorality. These practices were repugnant to the Romans—a people who delighted in watching gladiators and animals fight to the death in the arena. The fact that Christians refused to go to the arena, theaters, or public baths caused further suspicion. Also, Christians openly condemned homosexuality, a lifestyle considered normal in the Greco-Roman world. The lifestyles of Christians stood in sharp contrast to the scandalous lifestyles of many Romans, especially those in the upper classes. It is not surprising that Christians were persecuted in the Roman Empire.

ROMAN PERSECUTION

The persecution of Christians in the Roman Empire may be divided into two periods, from A.D. 64 to 250 and from 250 to 313. The first phase, which began with the persecution under Nero, was sporadic, local, and temporary. According to the Roman historians Tacitus and Seutonius, Nero (A.D. 54–68) launched a particularly brutal persecution of Christians in Rome and its environs in order to take suspicion off him for a fire that destroyed a portion of Rome. As mentioned earlier, the apostles Peter, Paul, and many other believers likely perished in this wave of persecution. In A.D. 95, Domitian (81–96), who took the title "master and god," launched a persecution that extended into the province of Asia. It is thought that those martyred under Domitian included one of his cousins and her husband. Ignatius, bishop of Antioch, suffered martyrdom during the reign of Trajan (98–117) in a persecution in Syria. Trajan was so impressed with the manner in which Christians died that he ordered anyone accused of being a Christian released if the individual would simply deny being a Christian.

After Trajan's reign, persecutions broke out during the reign of Antoninus Pius (137–161), during which Polycarp, the bishop of Smyrna was martyred, and again during the reign of Marcus Aurelius (161–180), a stoic philosopher and the last of the "five good emperors." By that time, increased barbarian pressure along the frontiers, internal revolt, and a particularly severe outbreak of the plague caused serious material and psychological stress to the empire. Blaming the Christians for Rome's troubles, Marcus Aurelius launched a persecution of Christians that was concentrated in North Africa and Egypt. Unlike Trajan, Marcus Aurelius was not impressed with the Christians' bravery. In his memoirs he attributes their bravery to total obstinacy, a far cry from what he considered the high courage of a Stoic sage.

With the reign of Decius (249–251) the persecutions took a new form. It became empirewide and a matter of state policy. The cause was in part the fact that the empire was obviously in decline. In a desperate attempt to unite the people, Decius issued an edict requiring everyone in the empire to make an annual offering to the genius of the emperor. In this way every citizen would demonstrate their loyalty. Some Christians either made the offering or otherwise obtained the required certificates saying that they had done so. Others, like Cyprian, the bishop of Carthage, went into hiding. Many chose martyrdom. How the Christian church dealt with those who abandoned the faith and later asked for readmission to the church became a serious issue.

The most severe persecution came in 303 during the reign of Diocletion (284–305). Not only were Christians ordered to make sacrifices to the pagan gods, but church buildings were destroyed and Christian writings were confiscated and burned. Again, the church had to decide how to respond to those who surrendered copies of the Scriptures out of fear for their lives and later asked to be readmitted to the church.

Before his retirement in 305, Diocletion undertook the first major revision of Roman government since the reign of Augustus. In a desperate attempt to keep the empire from collapsing, he divided the administration. There were two co-emperors, one in the West and one in the East, and two vice-emperors. When Diocletion and his co-emperor, Maximian, retired in 305, civil war broke out. By 311, the number of rivals for the throne was reduced to two, Constantine and Maxentius. In 312, on the eve of the battle of Milvian Bridge, Constantine was given a vision from God—the sign of the cross in the sky with the words, "In this sign conquer." Maxentius was defeated, and in 313, Constantine issued the Edict of Milan (named after the city from which he was ruling at the time), which granted "both to the

Christians and all others full authority to follow whatever worship each man has desired."

Whereas his predecessors saw Christianity as a threat to the empire's unity, Constantine saw it as a potential cement that could hold the empire together and even strengthen it. During his reign (he ruled with Licinius until 324, then alone until 337), Constantine showed favor to the Christian church. He issued edicts that restored church property confiscated during the persecution, granted financial support from state funds, exempted the clergy from taxation, and recognized Sunday as a day of worship. When controversies within the church threatened to disrupt the unity of the empire, Constantine called and presided over the councils of Arles (314) and Nicaea (325).

Constantine's edict of toleration was a milestone in the church's history. It raised obvious questions of the proper relationship between church and state, issues that became more important in 381, when Theodosius I declared Christianity the only legal religion in the Roman Empire. If a state is by definition Christian, then all that the state does is Christian. Wars, for example, become crusades——the armies battling for God or against him. Rather than the conscience of the state, the church becomes a department of state. In the eastern half of the empire (what later became known as the Byzantine Empire), a form of government evolved known as *caesaropapism,* where the emperor was head of both state and church. In the West, where central political authority vanished during the fifth century, the church remained independent of state control.

Constantine ended the persecution of the church and began a new era in church history. Church-state relations became an important issue from the fourth century on. Even more fundamental issues, however, were faced before Constantine's Edict of Milan. Christians found it necessary to answer the charges from Jewish and pagan writers, who put forth persuasive arguments against the true claims of Christianity. At the same time, there arose from within the church false teachings, or heresies. These sometimes resulted from attempts to defend some aspect of the faith from external (often pagan) philosophies or internal threats. A group of Christian writers from the end of the apostolic period until the middle of the fifth century took up their pens in defense of the faith. From the third century on, they were often referred to as the "church fathers."

DEFENDING THE FAITH
. . . .

In their defense of the faith, the church fathers helped to define orthodox belief through the formulation of creeds and a Christian theology. At the same time, they helped to shape the growth of the church and helped define the canon of the New Testament. How these developments interacted with one another is evident in the lives of several of the leading church fathers.

Clement of Rome (c. 30–c. 100), an elder in the church at Rome and, according to tradition, its fourth bishop, wrote in response to a dispute over authority. Several eventual developments in church structure are evident in Clement's letter to the Corinthian church. First is the distinction between laity and clergy. He was the first to use the term "layman." Second, Clement developed the idea of apostolic succession. The democratically elected elders and deacons derive their authority from God the Father, through Jesus Christ and the apostles. Finally, Clement emphasized obedience to the elders as a means of maintaining unity within the church.

Ignatius of Antioch (d.c. 117) boldly defended the true humanity of Jesus Christ against the heresy known as Docetism. The Docetists denied the Incarnation, holding that Christ's humanity was an illusion. To guard against such heresy and further the cause of unity, Ignatius was the first to emphasize the authority of one bishop in each congregation to whom the other elders and the rest of the congregation must submit. He also emphasized Communion, or the Eucharist, as a means of furthering unity in the local church. His model of a church governed by a "monarchical bishop," supported by elders and deacons, was generally accepted by the second century.

Justin Martyr (c. 100–165), who had flirted with various schools of classical philosophy, defended the faith against popular misconceptions by pagans and Jews. One of his pupils, Tatian (c. 110–c. 180), was the first to prepare a harmony of the Gospels in his *Diatessaron.* Athenagoras (second century) and Theophilus of Antioch (d. 180), both writing during the late-second century, described the Godhead as the Trinity. Theophilus is thought by some to have been the first to use the word *trias,* or Triad, in reference to God, although others accord that honor to Athenagoras. It was Tertullian (c. 155–c. 215), however, who first worked out the doctrine of the Trinity as three persons in one substance. Tertullian was also the first to formulate the doctrine of original sin.

Clement of Alexandria (c. 155–c. 215) felt Christians had nothing to fear from Greek philosophy, for Christianity was the most perfect philosophy. If Christianity could be destroyed by the reasoned arguments of the pagan philosophers, then Clement felt it should be destroyed. Clement was the first to use the word "clergy," or *kleros,* in reference to those who ministered full-time in the church. He is credited with having written the oldest known Christian hymn (outside of the New Testament), "Shepherd of Tender Youth."

In a sense, Clement of Alexandria foreshadowed the scholastic theologians of the High Middle Ages. He sought a reconciliation, or synthesis, of Christianity (revelation) and Greek philosophy (reason). Like Thomas Aquinas in the thirteenth century, Clement believed that all truth was God's truth, even if it was found in pagan philosophy. God's revelation took precedence, while the truth found in philosophy was designed to serve God.

Clement's desire to reconcile Christianity and philosophy introduced a problem that has continued to this day. His pupil, Origen (c. 185–c. 251), also introduced teachings that have continued to trouble the church. Origen was the most prolific of the church fathers and a leading scholar of the early church. He produced over two thousand works, only a small portion of which have survived. Among them is his *Hexapla,* six Hebrew and

Greek versions of the Old Testament set side by side in columns. He championed the allegorical method of interpreting Scripture—a method favored during the Middle Ages, but considered troublesome by many. In *De Principiis* (*On First Principles*), Origen presented the first systematic Christian theology, though not without serious errors. He did not hold to an orthodox view of the Trinity, as later defined at the Councils of Nicaea (325) and Chalcedon (451). Also, he believed in the preexistence of souls and universal salvation.

The Christian writer in the settled environment of the East tended to be preoccupied with theological issues. It was in the East that most heresies originated and were combated. In the West, Christian writers were more concerned with church polity, as might be expected in an environment where central civil authority was rapidly vanishing under pressure from barbarian invasions. By the third quarter of the fifth century, there was no imperial authority in the West. Those barbarians who were "Christians" (Goths and Lombards) were adherents of the Arian heresy. It fell upon Christians in the West to unify the church, and they largely did so by developing a monarchical church government centered in Rome. At this point, however, it should be noted that in the struggles over the heresies that emerged in the East, the Roman church demonstrated a gift for defining and expressing what was "orthodox." This was the case in the controversy over Arianism.

In the early church, Arianism was perhaps the most troublesome heresy that revolved around the Trinity. It raised questions regarding the relationship of the Son to the Father, the Holy Spirit to the Father in eternity, and between the human and divine natures in Jesus Christ. Monarchianism denied the Trinity by emphasizing the unity of the Godhead. It was condemned in 264 and 268 by synods held in Antioch. Apollinarianism denied Jesus Christ's full humanity and was condemned at the Council of Constantinople in 381. Nestorians, condemned at the Council of Chalcedon in 451, taught that Jesus Christ had two distinct natures, one human and one divine. Arianism was more influential in church history because it enjoyed imperial support at times and because a number of the Germanic tribes that settled in the West were converts to Arianism. Thus the Arians were a serious threat to orthodoxy as held by the Western church until the conversion of the Franks to the orthodox Christian faith in 496 (see chapter 2).

Arius (c. 250–336), a presbyter in the church at Alexandria, responded to what he felt was an overemphasis on the unity of the Godhead by teaching that the Son was a created being, "begotten by the Father." Only the Father was truly divine. The crucial issue was whether a Christ who was not divine could be the means of humanity's redemption. Alexander, Arius's bishop in Alexandria, had Arius condemned by a synod. However, Arius found significant support, including the bishop of Nicomedia. Heresies like Arianism threatened the unity of the church and also threatened the unity of the state. Therefore, Constantine called the first ecumenical council of the church.

The Council of Nicaea met in the summer of 325. Constantine, himself, presided over the most important session of the council, attended by 250 to 300 bishops. Arius's view that Jesus Christ was not coequal, coeternal, or of the same substance as God the Father was condemned as heretical by the council. The formula agreed to, which included the word *homoousius* (proposed by Constantine, meaning "same substance [of the Father]") was a clear rejection of Arianism. With later modifications it was approved at the fourth ecumenical Council of Chalcedon in 451 and became known as the Nicene Creed.

The Council of Nicaea marks the end of an era in church history. As noted by Mark Noll[2] and other church historians, the Council of Nicaea marks the end of the "pilgrim church," that is, the era when the church operated independently from the government. At Nicaea, the church in the East lost its independence. Henceforth, it was an established church, under imperial control. The church in the West, with its center at Rome, was more fortu-

[2] *Turning Points: Decisive Moments in the History of the Church* (Grand Rapids: Baker Books, 1997), 62-63.

nate. It was able to maintain its independence, but at the expense of creating a papal monarchy.

TIMELINE FOR CHAPTER 1

c. 30	Jesus Christ's crucifixion and resurrection
	Founding of the church at Pentecost
37	Stoning of Stephen
c. 49/50	Jerusalem Council
64	Persecution under Nero
	Peter and Paul martyred
70	Jewish revolt and the destruction of the temple
135	Bar Kochba's revolt and the fall of Jerusalem
313	Edict of Milan
325	Council of Nicaea
381	Theodosius I makes Christianity the state religion
	Council of Constantinople
382	Jerome begins Old Testament translation into Latin, the Vulgate Bible
397	Synod of Carthage agrees on New Testament canon

CHAPTER 2

The Rise of Christendom: The Church in the Middle Ages

THE BIG PICTURE

During the fifth century, Roman authority in Europe gave way to an era of barbarian chieftains fighting over pieces of former Roman real estate. In 410, Rome was sacked by the Goths, and in 476 the last Roman emperor in the West was deposed by a German chieftain. During the ensuing four or five centuries, Roman civilization all but disappeared, as cities vanished and illiteracy became the rule. In the midst of the chaos, the Western church converted the barbarians and synthesized classical civilization with Christianity, forming a new worldview that became the foundation of medieval civilization. The task was accomplished through the creation of the papacy as the central authority of Western Christianity, the rise of monasticism, and the assertion of orthodox doctrine by the ecumenical councils of the church, especially Nicaea (325) and Chalcedon (451). The rise of the papacy also increased emphasis on the sacraments and tradition, establishing the institutional church as a necessary intermediary between the believer and God.

KEY EVENTS

410   Augustine, bishop of Hippo, writes *The City of God,* the first Christian philosophy of history, in response to news that Rome has been sacked by the Visigoths.

420	Benedict of Nursia founds a monastery at Monte Casino in Italy that will become the model for Western monasticism.
451	The Council of Chalcedon adopts the Nicene Creed, first formulated at the Council of Nicaea in 325, as the definition of orthodox belief.
476	Christians in the West look to the pope in Rome for leadership as the fall of the Roman Empire in the West is supplanted by Christendom, i.e., Christ's kingdom.
664	The Irish Celtic church and the Roman Catholic church, the two orthodox Christian churches in the West, unite under the authority of Rome at the Synod of Whitby.

In 409, the Arian "Christian" king of the Visigoths, Alaric, laid siege to the city of Rome. Twice the citizens paid a ransom, but twice Alaric returned. During the siege, many barbarian slaves escaped from the city and joined Alaric's army. Then, in August of 410, the gates of Rome were opened by an anonymous slave and Goths poured into the city. Only the churches of St. Peter and St. Paul were spared—all else was subjected to the wrath of the barbarians. Rome, the eternal city, capital of the greatest empire in history, was captured.

When news of Rome's fall reached Augustine, bishop of Hippo, across the Mediterranean Sea in North Africa, he was shocked. For Augustine, as for most educated Romans of the early-fifth century, it was difficult to conceive a world without the Roman Empire. For centuries it seemed as though the whole purpose of history was to be found in the rise and dominance of Roman civilization. Since Constantine, Rome's mission had been the Christianization of the classical world. Indeed, although Rome had not been the political capital of the empire since the reign of Diocletian, it had become the capital of Christ's kingdom.

Augustine sought to answer the question of why God would allow the barbarians, pagans, and heretics to sack his city. Pagan intellectuals contributed the decline of the empire to the spread of Christianity, which brought down the wrath of the ancient gods. But as the Roman Empire faded away in the West, the church took its place. Roman provincial governors were replaced by bishops. The emperor was replaced by the bishop of Rome, the one to whom, according to the Petrine Theory, Jesus Christ had given the keys to heaven and hell. The church, it seemed, had triumphed over the pagan empire. Why, then, would God allow his eternal city to be sacked?

To answer that question, Augustine wrote the *City of God,* the first Christian philosophy of history. For Augustine, history is not an endless repetition of fatalistic cycles from which there is no escape. History, rather, is the story of God's wondrous acts. From Creation to the coming of Jesus Christ, and from his death and resurrection to his glorious return at the end of time, there is a flow to history. Thus Augustine provided a Scriptural framework by which Christians from the fifth century forward could understand what was happening around them. Augustine died in 430 as another barbarian tribe, the Vandals, was besieging Hippo.

In 452, Rome was threatened by Attila the Hun. He was referred to as "the Scourge of God" by Christians. Leo I, bishop of Rome from 440 to 461, met Attila on the banks of the Mincio River in northern Italy and persuaded him to turn away from Rome. After this Attila's army was stricken by a severe epidemic, and he turned north into Gaul (modern France), where he died the following year. Leo I was less successful with the Arian "Christian" Vandals. In 455, the Vandals crossed over from North Africa and attacked Rome. Leo I was still able to convince their leader, Gaiseric, not to burn the city, but in exchange, the Vandals were allowed to sack the city for two weeks. They looted the city more thoroughly than their Gothic brothers did in 409. A sense of what happened may be gleaned from the resulting word, "vandalism."

After Augustine's death, Europe faced six hundred years of barbarian invasions. During that period, often called the Dark Ages, civilization virtually disappeared in the West. Europe remained under siege for more than five hundred years as barbarian armies battled one another for territory. Central government disappeared, and in its place grew independent Germanic kingdoms, staking out territory like modern gangs in the ruins of inner cities. Learning and books, too, all but vanished. Where there are no schools, literacy soon dies out; and the illiterate do not treasure books.

Many historians believe that civilization survived the long night from the end of the fifth to the eleventh century largely due to the efforts of the church. When the Roman Empire fell in the West, the church possessed a uniform system of belief summed up in the Apostles' Creed and the Nicene Creed. By the end of the fourth century, the canon of the New Testament was agreed upon and formally accepted at the Synod of Rome (382) and the Synod of Carthage (397). By the reign of Leo I, the bishop of Rome was generally recognized in the West as the supreme head of the church. Monasticism spread from the East to the West during the second half of the fourth century. Through all these means—creeds, canon, pope, and monks—the Christian church tamed and converted the barbarians, synthesized classical civilization with Christianity, and provided a new worldview that became the foundation of a new, medieval civilization. This was "Christendom."

THE RISE OF THE PAPACY

The dominant role played by the church during the Middle Ages earned the period the epitaph "Age of Faith." The church was such an all-pervasive influence in part because of the emergence of the pope as the *de facto* monarch of Christendom. The rise of the papacy during the Middle Ages was due to a variety of reasons. First, there were theological arguments drawn from Scripture, such as the Petrine Theory (the theory that the bishop of Rome, as successor to Peter, was the head of the church, since the keys of the Kingdom were given to him) and apostolic succession. There were also what might be called historical accidents, if indeed there is such a thing. As time unfolded, Rome emerged as the focus of power and historical continuity in the

West. It was, in fact, the only surviving apostolic city after the rise of Islam and the decline of the Byzantine Empire.

As noted previously, the theory of apostolic succession was developed by Clement of Rome near the end of the first century. Both Irenaeus and Tertullian, two of the four Ante-Nicene Fathers (Origen and Clement of Alexandria were the other two) espoused the doctrine in their writings. The belief that the apostles possessed authority which they passed on to their successors led to the logical conclusion that Peter's authority was perpetuated in the bishops of Rome. According to the Petrine Theory, that authority was the "power of the keys," or the authority to act as Christ's vicar on earth.

The Petrine Theory was based upon an incident described in Matthew 16:13-19. Jesus asked his disciples who the people thought he was. Jesus then asked the disciples, "Who do you say I am?" It was Peter who responded: "You are the Christ, the Son of the living God." Jesus then informed Peter that the truth he had just spoken was not the result of logical reasoning, but divine revelation. Jesus then went on to say, "And I tell you that you are Peter, and on this rock I will build my church, and the gates of Hades will not overcome it. I will give you the keys of the kingdom of heaven; whatever you bind on earth will be bound in heaven, and whatever you loose on earth will be loosed in heaven" (Matthew 16:18-19).[3]

The crucial word in these verses is, of course, the "rock" upon which Jesus said he would build his church. For Christians in the West, the "rock" was increasingly understood to be Peter, the man, not the revelation he voiced.

According to church tradition, Peter founded the church in Rome. Peter is identified as the first bishop of Rome in the earliest known list of Roman bishops compiled by Irenaeus. Damasus, bishop of Rome from 366 to 384, was the first to claim the authority given to Peter. He was also the first to refer to Rome as the Apostolic See (the "seat of the apostle"). Other measures taken by Damasus to enhance the position of the

---

[3] Other verses used to support the Petrine Theory are Luke 22:32 and John 21:15-17.

bishop of Rome were to encourage pilgrimages to Rome, the veneration of martyrs, the adoption of Latin as the liturgical language, and the commissioning of Jerome to prepare a new Latin translation of the Bible. Jerome's translation, the Vulgate, became the authoritative Bible for the Western church.

Innocent I (401–417) claimed the authority to act as supreme arbiter in doctrinal disputes within the church, East and West. Leo I, "the Great" (440–461), appealed to the Petrine Theory in defense of his claim to supreme authority, stating, "To deny the pope is to deny Peter; to deny Peter is to deny Christ."[4] Leo I's assertion that Peter speaks through the bishop of Rome was given support by the Council of Chalcedon (451). Leo I's position on the nature of Jesus Christ as one person in two natures was accepted by the council as orthodox. In doing so, the council said, "Peter has spoken through Leo."

The Petrine Theory implies that the bishop of Rome is in effect the "vicar of Christ." It was Gelasius I (492–496) who first used the title. Siricius (384–399) was the first to use the title "pope," but it was not used exclusively for the bishop of Rome until the eleventh century. Gelasius I also claimed the right to ratify the acts of church councils and expounded the theory of the two swords. According to this theory, God has ordained two authorities in the world, one ecclesiastical and the other secular. When in conflict, the secular must submit to the ecclesiastical, for it is the church—ultimately the bishop of Rome—that possesses the power of the keys of the kingdom of heaven.

Gregory I, "the Great" (590–604), is often considered the first medieval pope. Along with Ambrose (c. 339–397), Augustine, and Jerome (c. 347–420), Gregory is one of the four great fathers of the Western church. Gregory was a fine, humble man who saw himself as the "servant of the servants of God." A good administrator, he made the Roman bishopric the wealthiest in the church and used the income to finance the government of Rome, care for the city's poor, and buy off the Lombards, who threat-

[4] Quoted in Robert G. Clouse, Richard V. Pierard, and Edwin M. Yamauchi, *Two Kingdoms: The Church and Culture Through the Ages* (Chicago: Moody Press, 1993), 140.

ened Rome. He was a popular preacher, whose sermons emphasized humility and piety. A prolific writer, Gregory's *Pastoral Care* was one of the most widely read religious books of the Middle Ages and the standard pastor's handbook.

Gregory I enhanced the authority of the papacy and placed his stamp upon medieval theology. He asserted authority over the whole church and expanded Christianity in Europe by sending missionaries out to England and Spain. Among his most influential theological views was his belief that each person possesses a free will and has inherited Adam's sin but not his guilt. Gregory did not see God's grace as irresistible, but he believed God predestined the elect to salvation based upon his foreknowledge and the merits of individuals. Gregory believed in the verbal inspiration of the Bible but held church tradition to be its equal. Since people must merit God's grace to some degree, Gregory emphasized good works and encouraged the veneration of relics and the use of images as aids in strengthening faith. Gregory also provided the chief medieval defense of the doctrine of purgatory.

The authority of the papacy was enhanced further by the increasing distinction between the laity and the clergy. This was shown by the necessity of the clergy to perform the sacraments through which God's Grace is dispensed to the believer. During the first century there were no priests whose function was to minister a sacramental system, for every believer was his or her own "priest," with direct access to God through Jesus Christ. There were only two sacraments, baptism and the Lord's Supper, neither of which were considered the means of salvation.

By the end of the sixth century there were seven sacraments—Communion, baptism, confirmation, penance, extreme unction, ordination, and marriage. Since Grace (i.e., salvation) was dispensed through the sacraments and a special class of priests with authority to minister them was required, an intermediator (or obstacle) between the individual and God was created. The Christian could not exist apart from the institutional church, for the church alone possessed the authority to minister the essential sacraments. According to the Petrine Theory, that

authority emanated from the pope through the clergy. To suggest
a return to the priesthood of believers of the early church, as
Luther and the sixteenth-century Reformers would do, was to
threaten the very foundation of the medieval church. If the individual believer has direct access to God, then the special class of
priests are not needed, thus undermining the whole hierarchy of
the medieval church from the Supreme Pontiff down to the parish priest.

THE RISE OF MONASTICISM

Some historians believe that Christianity in the West survived
not solely due to the rise and influence of the papacy, but also
because of monasticism. From the chaos of the early Middle
Ages until the emergence of the nation-states during the fifteenth
and sixteenth centuries, they were the only two institutions capa-
ble of providing meaningful leadership. The influence of the papacy waxed and waned, depending upon the strength of the
individual popes and the secular rulers who opposed them.

Monasticism first appeared along the desert fringe in Egypt
and Syria during the late-third and early-fourth centuries. Early
monasticism was *anchoritic,* that is, individuals living as hermits. By the end of the fourth century, the deserts of the Near
East were teeming with hermit monks. During the latter part of
the fourth century, monasticism spread to the West. At first, the
monks in the West were hermits, too; but since the environment
did not favor such harsh asceticism, *cenobitic,* or communal,
monasticism became the rule.

There were a variety of reasons for the appearance of monasticism. Certainly one was the view that there was an inherent conflict between the flesh and spirit. This originated, in part, in
Greek philosophy. The spirit was good; the material was evil.
Many felt the need to separate themselves from a society and
church that was becoming corrupted by material excess. The
rapid growth of the church brought many pagans into the church
that were only superficially converted, at best. It is estimated that

at the time of Constantine (the early-fourth century) 10 percent of the population professed to be Christian. A century later, the number had risen to 90 percent. This influx of nominal converts led to a lessening of religious zeal and the introduction of semi-pagan practices, some of which were reflected in the corruption of church doctrine and institutions.

As noted above, the legalization of Christianity by Constantine had both positive and negative results. Tolerance led to the end of martyrdom, at least within the "Christian" empire, but it also led to the union of church and state in the East. For some, martyrdom was replaced by asceticism. The monks, especially the more eccentric hermits in the East, became the new martyrs. In a sense, anyone could become a martyr to the faith by renouncing the world and becoming a monk.

As the church grew in numbers, congregations with church buildings replaced the house churches of the first century. At the same time the emergence of the monarchical bishop and the sacramental system contributed to an emphasis on corporate worship. Again, choosing to become a monk was one way of returning to an individualistic mode of worship.

No one knows for sure who was the first monk. Anthony of Egypt (c. 251–356) is regarded as the founder of anchoritic monasticism. Our knowledge of him comes largely from a biography, *The Life of Anthony,* written by Athanasius of Alexandria (c. 300–373). According to Athanasius, Anthony was a well-to-do Coptic peasant from Egypt, who took to heart Jesus' advice to the rich young man: "If you want to be perfect, go, sell your possessions and give to the poor, and you will have treasure in heaven. Then come, follow me" (Matthew 19:21). Around the age of twenty, Anthony sold all of his possessions, gave the proceeds to the poor, and became a hermit. He spent twenty years alone in a ruined fort in the Egyptian desert near the Red Sea. There he fasted, gave up bathing, put on a hair shirt, and devoted himself to a life of prayer, Bible study, meditation, and battling real or imagined demons. As his fame spread, others went to live near him as hermits. Constantine and two of his sons wrote to

Anthony seeking the advice of this monk with no formal education. Anthony died in 356 at 105 years of age.

The extreme austerities of some of the more famous hermits would likely be considered evidence of mental illness, today, but at the time, these practices earned them the title "athletes of God." One such monk was Simeon Stylites. After spending ten years alone in a cell near Antioch, Simeon spent several months buried up to his neck. He then mounted a sixty-foot pillar, where he spent the next thirty years sitting on a platform only three feet in diameter. By the time of his death in 459, it was said that his legs had become putrefied to the point where they dripped with vermin. In the meantime, his advice was sought by pilgrims and emperors alike and even by the Councils of Ephesus (431) and Chalcedon (451).

Pillar saints became a common sight after Simeon. Others sought holiness through even more bizarre practices. Some lived off grass like cattle. Others confined themselves to cells so small they could neither stand nor lie down full length. An abhorrence for cleanliness was characteristic of such hermit monks. One notable example was Ammoun, who never undressed or bathed after becoming a hermit. Another, named Abraham, did not wash his face for fifty years. Some monks refused to wash or cut their hair, except at Easter. Such fanaticism was more characteristic of Eastern monasticism and was seldom found in the West.

Although not unknown in the East (where it began in 320 with Pachomius), communal monasticism was the form that took root and flourished in the West. In an environment where almost everyone lacked material comforts and where the climate was much harsher, anchoritic monasticism had little appeal. Communal organization was necessary. Also, such monasticism in the West enjoyed the support of Ambrose, Augustine, and Martin of Tours.

Perhaps the leading pioneer of monasticism in the West was Martin of Tours (c. 316–c. 397), a former soldier. After his conversion, Martin tried to become a hermit but in 372 was forced by the Christians in Tours to become their bishop. A humble man, Martin continued to live in a cell next to the church and always refused to sit on the bishop's throne, preferring a stool. His growing popularity led him to retreat to Marmoutier, where he founded the first monastery in Gaul. A contemporary biography says of him, "Nothing was in his mouth except Christ, nothing in his heart but piety, peace, and pity."[5] After Martin's death, numerous churches were dedicated to him, and he became the first non-martyr canonized by the church.

Another pioneer of Western monasticism was John Cassian, who founded monasteries for both men and women in 415 at Marseilles in southern Gaul. Soon thousands were enrolled. Cassian reacted against the dangers of extreme asceticism. He wrote a rule book, *Institutes,* giving monks detailed instructions for the monasteries he founded. Cassian also collected his conversations with the desert monks and published them as *Collations.* These two books were very popular and influential throughout the Middle Ages, and they are still read today.

From Gaul, monasticism spread to Ireland in the late-fifth and early-sixth centuries. It is not known for certain who founded the Irish church. Credit has traditionally been given to Patrick (c. 389–461), the son of Christian parents in Roman Britain. Patrick was seized by Celtic raiders at the age of sixteen and was sold as a slave in Ireland. After six years of slavery, during which he became a Christian, Patrick escaped. After studying in a monastery in Gaul, he returned to Ireland in 432, already consecrated a bishop.

The Ireland of Patrick's day was a tribal society. In the absence of towns, the Irish church was a monastic church. The monasteries Patrick established were comprised of clusters of monks living in individual mud huts under the authority of an abbot appointed by the local clan chief, or king. As the Irish turned to Christianity, the monks took the position in Irish society previously occupied by the Druids. The Druids functioned as scholars, priests, and magicians. They were the "learned" elite in an illiterate society.

---

[5] Quoted in Kenneth Scott Latourette, *A History of Christianity* (New York: Harper & Row, 1953), 231.

Irish monasticism was known for its emphasis on scholarship. Indeed, Ireland was the center of literacy and Christian culture during the dark age of the barbarian conquest of the continent. Some modern scholars go so far as to credit the Irish monks with having saved Christian civilization in the West.[6] It fell upon the Irish monks to preserve from extinction the Latin literature of classical civilization.

The definitive form of Western monasticism was provided by Benedict of Nursia. After a brief stint as a hermit, Benedict founded a monastery at Monte Cassino, near Naples, around 420. Benedict envisioned the monastery as a completely self-contained, self-supporting, and self-governing world of its own. There was to be no contact with the world outside the monastery. An abbot, elected for life by the monks, had absolute authority over the monks, who took a vow of lifetime obedience to the abbot. Life in the monastery was characterized by a communal life of absolute regularity, strict discipline, and unvarying routine.

Benedict drew up a *Rule* for the monastery. There was to be none of the mortification of the flesh that characterized the lives of the desert hermits. In fact, each monk was made responsible for his brother monks to see that each ate regular meals and to see that special care was given to the elderly, the sick, and the young. Silence was not required, but idle talk was discouraged. Bathing, considered a luxury, was discouraged. Later, Benedictine monasteries in England allowed the monks to take three or four baths per year. Benedict devised a daily routine that prescribed four hours of communal liturgical prayer and worship; four hours of private meditation, prayer, and reading; six hours of physical labor; and ten hours reserved for eating and sleeping.

Gregory the Great's biography of Benedict popularized Benedict's order and encouraged its growth. By the end of the ninth

[6] See, for example, Thomas Cahill, *How the Irish Saved Civilization: The Untold Story of Ireland's Heroic Role from the Fall of Rome to the Rise of Medieval Europe* (New York; Doubleday, 1995).

A MONK'S DAY ACCORDING TO ST. BENEDICT

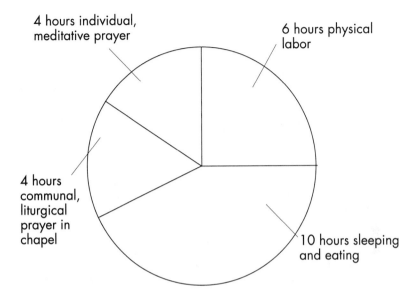

4 hours individual, meditative prayer

6 hours physical labor

4 hours communal, liturgical prayer in chapel

10 hours sleeping and eating

century the *Rule* of Benedict became the basic rule for all Western monasteries, except those in Ireland. By that time, however, the monasteries were no longer self-sustaining units. Often the monks, drawn from the nobility, devoted themselves to education and the liturgy, while serfs supported them with their labor. Increasingly, the monasteries became educational centers from which scholars were recruited to serve as bishops and popes or in the secular state as royal chancellors and advisers. It has been conservatively estimated that 90 percent of the literate population between 600 and 1100 were educated in monastic schools.

Education and the preservation of literacy and literature was one of the primary services of the monasteries, though this was not originally intended by Benedict. Nearly all of the earliest known copies of classical literature are copies made by the medieval monks. Another major service provided by the medieval monks was their efforts at Christianizing the pagan barbarians who occupied Europe at the end of the Roman Empire.

EARLY MEDIEVAL MISSIONS

The migration of the Germanic tribes into the western Roman Empire during the late-fourth and fifth centuries after the fall of the empire presented the church in the West with a formidable task. The barbarians had to be both Christianized (i.e., converted) and civilized. The former was often quickly, if only superficially, achieved by the conversion of individual rulers, who in turn ordered their subjects baptized, as well. Civilizing the barbarians, themselves, was a much more difficult task and took centuries to accomplish.

Evangelizing the barbarian Germans was not simply a matter of converting pagans. Most of the Germanic kingdoms that existed at the end of the fifth century were Arian "Christian," rather than purely pagan. The Vandals, Goths, and Lombards were all Arian. Significantly, the tribe that was to prove most important, the Franks, was pagan. Clovis (c. 466–511) took the title "King of the Franks" after conquering the area between the Seine and Loire Rivers. In 496, Clovis converted to the Christian (Roman) faith of his wife, a Burgundian princess. On Christmas Day, 496, Clovis and three thousand of his warriors were baptized.

What was particularly significant about the conversion of the Franks was that they converted to orthodox Christianity, not the Arian heresy. This proved to be beneficial for both Clovis and the Roman church. For the Franks, it meant they had the support of the Roman and Christian native population. Other German tribes were viewed as heretics. For the Roman church, it meant the beginning of a centuries-long cooperation between the kings of France and the papacy.

A major mission effort was undertaken by the Celtic church during the sixth and seventh centuries. Irish monks, called "White Martyrs" because of their white woolen robes, founded monasteries in Scotland, England, Belgium, Germany, France, and even Italy. The monasteries they founded (e.g., Iona, Lindesfarne, Luxiel) became centers of both evangelism and culture. Columba and Aidan carried Christianity to Scotland. Columbanus and his followers went to France, Switzerland, and northern Italy. More than two hundred monasteries were founded by Irish monks in France alone.

Meanwhile, missionary monks were being sent out by the Roman church, as well. In 596, Gregory I sent Augustine, a prior of a monastery in Rome, to the kingdom of Kent in England to evangelize the Anglo-Saxons. In 597, Gregory appointed Augustine the first archbishop of England. In 625, when the daughter of the Christian king of Kent went to Northumbria to marry its king, Edwin, he was converted, and York became the second center of the English church.

Upon the death of Edwin, Oswald (c. 605–641), a Celtic Christian, became king of Northumbria. Celtic and Roman Christianity, both orthodox, came face-to-face in Britain. Their differences, though minor by modern standards, were very serious matters in the seventh century. They differed on how to ordain bishops, how to shave the head of monks, and most importantly, on how to calculate the date of Easter. A synod was convened at the Abby of Whitby in Northumbria in 664 to resolve the differences. The king of Northumbria ruled in favor of the Roman monks, when the Irish monks admitted that Peter, the founder of the church at Rome, was superior to Columba. In short, the Roman church possessed a superior set of relics. The Celtic church submitted to the authority of the pope.

Other monks carried the gospel to other parts of Europe. Boniface (680–754), an Anglo-Saxon monk, evangelized parts of Germany. He was the first to employ women as missionaries. Between 568 and 675, the Lombards renounced Arianism and embraced the true faith. The Arian Visigoths in Spain did likewise in 589, following the conversion of their king. The area of modern Belgium and Holland was converted in 690. By 800, when the Frankish king Charlemagne was crowned "Emperor of

ECUMENICAL CHURCH COUNCILS

Council of Nicaea (325) — *Called by Emperor Constantine* — Declared the divinity of God the Son to be of one substance and one nature with that of God the Father. Original version of the Nicene Creed.

Council of Constantinople (381) — *Called by Theodosius I* — Affirmed deity of Holy Spirit. Nicene Creed altered to affirm that Holy Spirit proceeds from both the Father and the Son.

Council of Ephesus (431) — *Called by Theodosius II* — Condemned Nestorian teaching of two natures in Jesus Christ, and by implication affirmed Jesus Christ as God-man.

Council of Chalcedon (451) — *Called by Marcian* — Affirmed Jesus Christ as "truly God and truly man" having "two natures, without confusion, without change, without division, without separation."

Council of Constantinople (553) — *Called by Justinian* — Affirmed the conclusions of the Council of Ephesus (431) and Chalcedon (451)

Council of Constantinople (680–681) — *Called by Constantine IV* — Proclaimed unity of divine and human wills in Jesus Christ, with human will subject to divine will.

Council of Nicaea (787) — *Called by Constantine V's widow* — Legitimatized veneration of images, emphasizing honor is due only to what they represent, not to the images themselves.

the Romans," most of western Europe and the British Isles acknowledged the authority of the papacy.

TIMELINE FOR CHAPTER 2

410	Visigoths sack Rome
413–426	Augustine writes *City of God*
430	Hippo falls to Vandals
431	Council of Ephesus
432	Patrick begins conversion of Ireland
440–461	Leo I (appeals to Petrine Theory)
451	Council of Chalcedon
452	Attila the Hun turned away from Rome by Leo I
527	Dionysius Exiguus introduces the chronological notation "A.D."
528	Justinian begins codification of Roman law
529	Benedict of Nursia founds monastery at Monte Cassino
596	Gregory I sends Augustine to Kent (England) to convert Angles
622	Mohammed established as religious and political leader in Medina
664	Synod of Whitby
754	Donation of Pepin creates future Papal States
800	Charlemagne crowned "Emperor of the Romans"

CHAPTER THREE

Christendom: The Church in the High Middle Ages

THE BIG PICTURE

During the ninth through the eleventh centuries, the period known as the High Middle Ages, the church in the West reached its peak of power and influence. The brief unification of western Europe under Charlemagne enabled the church to Christianize much of Europe and consolidate its authority under royal patronage. The collapse of Charlemagne's empire following his death plunged Europe into feudal anarchy, made all the worse by the Viking invasions. Feudalism fueled the spiritual decline of the church by submitting it to the control of local secular lords, who exploited its wealth and influence. In the early-tenth century, a reform movement aimed at freeing the church from secular control arose among the Cluniac monks. These reformers captured the papacy in 1073 with the election of Gregory VII. A showdown between Gregory VII and the Holy Roman Emperor Henry IV resulted in the triumph of the church over secular interests. Under Innocent III, the papacy came closest to achieving the goal of Christendom, Christ's kingdom, as an absolute monarchy under the authority of the pope. The consolidation of papal power led to a final split between the church in the West and the church in the East in 1054.

KEY EVENTS

800   The Christianization of pagan Europe by the orthodox Roman Catholic church goes forward under patronage

of the Frankish kings, especially during the reign of Charlemagne, crowned "Emperor of the Romans" on Christmas Day.

1054   Disputes over papal claims and forms of worship lead to the permanent split in Christianity between the Roman Catholic (Latin) church and the Greek Orthodox church.

1095   Pope Urban II launches the Crusades (1095–1291) at the Council of Clermont, thus renewing contacts between Europe and the Middle East.

1215   The Fourth Lateran Council makes transubstantiation official dogma, thus elevating the Mass to a sacrifice.

On Christmas day in the year 800, Charlemagne (c. 742–814), king of the Franks, attended mass in St. Peter's Basilica in Rome. As he knelt before the tomb of the apostle to pray, Pope Leo III (795–816) placed a crown upon his head. Then all those present in the church shouted three times in unison: "To Charles Augustus, crowned by God, great and peace-giving emperor, life and victory." It was one of the most significant events in European history and a very important moment in the history of Christianity.

Charlemagne's coronation was significant for several reasons. First, there was once again an emperor in the West for the first time since 476 (although it was not until 813 that the Byzantine emperor recognized Charlemagne's use of the title). Charlemagne established his rule over much of the former Roman Empire in Europe. Northern Italy, what is now modern France, the Low Countries, and Germany were part of his empire. Also, it is significant that it was the pope who placed the crown on Charlemagne's head. This symbolized that his authority to rule came from God, affirmed by God's representative on earth, the pope. Just as Samuel in the Old Testament anointed Saul as God's chosen king of Israel, so, too, did Leo III crown Charlemagne.

THE FRANCO-PAPAL ALLIANCE

The coronation of Charlemagne cemented an alliance between the papacy and the Frankish kings begun with the conversion of

Clovis in 496. By the middle of the eighth century, real power in the Frankish kingdom was held by a royal official known as the Mayor of the Palace. In 732, when the victorious armies of Islam crossed the Pyrenees into France, the Mayor of the Palace was Charlemagne's grandfather, Charles Martel (Charles the Hammer, c. 690–741). The Franks, under Charles, met and defeated the Muslim army at Tours on the Loire River. Historians dispute the military significance of the victory, but what is certain is that throughout the Middle Ages, Charles Martel and the Franks were credited with having saved Christendom from conquest by Islam.

Charles Martel was succeeded by his son Pepin III (741–768), also known as Pepin the Short, or Pepin the Great. Like his father before him, Pepin supported the missionary work of Boniface among the Germans west of the Rhine. Acting with authority from Pope Zacharias (741–752), Boniface anointed and crowned Pepin king of the Franks in 751. In 753, when the independence of the papacy was threatened by the Lombards, Pope Stephen II (752–757) crossed the Alps and appealed to Pepin for help. Pepin was once again anointed and crowned king of the Franks, this time by the pope himself. Stephen II also conferred upon Pepin and his sons the title "Patrician of the Romans," forbidding the Franks upon pain of excommunication from ever choosing a king not of Pepin's descent.

In 756, Pepin invaded Italy, defeated the Lombards, and gave to Stephen II all of the territories in central Italy formerly belonging to the Byzantine Empire. This grant of territory to the papacy, known as the Donation of Pepin, later became the Papal States. It was a mixed blessing for the papacy. Having a territory to rule, the pope was independent of any secular ruler. However, the pope was also forced to wear two hats, one spiritual and one political. The ethical conflict must have been obvious.

Charlemagne continued and deepened the relationship between the church and the kingdom. His coronation signified the birth of a new "Christian" empire. The papacy had turned away from its dependence upon the emperor in Constantinople and looked north to the new imperial capital in Aachen

(Aix-la-Chapelle) as the axis of Christendom. Church historian Mark A. Noll correctly summarizes the significance of Charlemagne's coronation when he observes:

> For the next 800 years and more, the politics, learning, social organization, art, music, economics, and law of Europe would be "Christian"—not necessarily in the sense of fully incorporating norms of the gospel, but because the fate of the Western church centered in Rome had been so decisively linked with the new "Roman" emperor over the Alps.[7]

The synthesis of Judeo-Christianity, classical civilization, and the Germanic traditions was finally complete. The result was what is called Western, or European, civilization. Christianity and Western civilization became increasingly synonymous. This confusion of identities would become increasingly problematic for the spread of the gospel, as Europe began to "discover" the rest of the world at the close of the Middle Ages.

Charlemagne recognized the symbolic significance of allowing himself to be crowned by the pope. Charlemagne was a pious Christian who attended Mass every morning and Vespers every evening. He took a sincere interest in the welfare of the church and continued the reforms begun by his father. He strengthened the system of archbishops, who supervised the bishops. The bishops exercised discipline over the clergy. Both bishops and clergy were supported by a system of tithes. Charlemagne stressed the education of the clergy and even instructed them in what they were to preach and how to baptize. In general, his reforms stressed conformity and centralization based upon the Roman model.

Charlemagne's interest in educational reform led him to found a palace school at Aachen. He sent to York, the cultural center of Western Christendom at the time, for the Anglo-Saxon scholar,

[7] *Turning Points*, 121.

Alcuin. Charlemagne commissioned Alcuin to oversee his school, and under Alcuin's tutelage, the palace school became the nucleus of an intellectual and cultural revival known as the Carolingian Renaissance. Monks were put to work copying (and thus preserving) the Latin classics. From the palace school, monks were sent out to revive the monastic and cathedral schools.

This intellectual revival also stimulated theological discourse. Western theologians wrote about the "errors of the Greeks." The debate over the use of images (icons) and the inclusion of the phrase "and the Son" (the *Filioque*) in the Nicene Creed by western Christians were two issues that encouraged the growing divide between the church in the West and the East. Theological debates of the later Middle Ages were anticipated by theologians of the Carolingian period. The questions of Mary's perpetual virginity, "double predestination" (i.e., that God has predestined some to salvation and some to condemnation), and the "real presence" of Christ's body and blood in the Eucharist (transubstantiation) were all discussed by Carolingian theologians. Indeed, the first teaching on "double predestination" and the first clearly formulated statement on transubstantiation appeared during the Carolingian Renaissance.

Charlemagne's empire was not a true revival of the ancient Roman Empire, whatever the people of the time may have thought. There was not the economic revival—no rebirth of trade, commerce, or banking—that had characterized the urban empire of the Romans. Charlemagne's empire was a vast area temporarily held together by the force of his personality. Those within the empire gave personal loyalty to Charlemagne. There was no revival of the Roman concept of a state, as summed up in the motto, "The Senate and People of Rome." Such concepts were totally foreign to the German mind in the ninth century.

FEUDALISM AND THE DECLINE OF THE CHURCH
. . . .

Charlemagne died on January 28, 814. According to Einhard (his biographer and one of his court scholars), eclipses and earthquakes marked the approach of Charlemagne's death. In accordance with Teutonic custom, in 806 Charlemagne made provision for the partition of his empire among his three sons, Pepin, Charles, and Louis. By 811, only Louis remained alive. In an elaborate ceremony at the palace in Aachen in 813, Charlemagne crowned his only surviving son Louis, "Emperor and Augustus." Upon Charlemagne's death, his empire passed intact to Louis.

Louis the Pious (778–840) was not a warrior king like his father. Louis did not dominate the church as his father had done. He allowed himself to be crowned by the pope, something his father advised him against, again giving credence to the pope's claim to the authority to decide who should wear the imperial crown. Unable to control either his three sons or his nobles, Louis's reign was marked by civil war. Upon his death in 840, his two younger sons, Charles the Bald (c. 823–877) and Louis the German (c. 822–876), united against their brother Lothair (c. 795–855), who inherited the imperial title and a thin strip of territory from the North Sea to Italy, known as the "Middle Kingdom."

Lothair's kingdom was divided among his three sons upon his death in 855. Weak Carolingian kings continued to rule until 887 in France and 911 in Germany. The imperial title passed out of use in 924, having been possessed by petty Italian kinglets for several decades. The imperial title, together with the vision of a universal Christian empire, was revived in 962 when Pope John XII crowned the Saxon duke Otto I the first Holy Roman Emperor.

The fragmentation of Charlemagne's empire was accompanied by new waves of invasions. From the ninth to the eleventh century, Europe was attacked from the south by the Muslims, from the east by the Magyars, and from the north by the Vikings. The Muslims occupied Sicily, Corsica, and Sardinia in the Mediterranean Sea, and the Rhone River delta in southern France. They also established bases in Italy. In 846, the Muslims threatened Rome and plundered the churches of St. Peter and St. Paul. The Magyars came from central Asia and settled in the area of modern Hungary. From there they raided throughout Germany and eastern France until their defeat in 955 by Otto at the battle of the Lechfield.

The most devastating raids were those of the Vikings, or Northmen, from Scandinavia. The Vikings first attacked Britain in the summer of 787. By the early 800s, the monasteries of Lindisfarne and Jarrow, the cultural centers of Christendom in Britain, had been burned. For the next two centuries the Vikings raided the river valleys of Europe. Monasteries and churches were looted of their treasures, the clergy slaughtered, sometimes nailed to the church doors, and the buildings burned. "From the fury of the Northmen, O Lord deliver us," was a prayer heard throughout Christendom during that dark age.

There was no longer a central government and no great warrior like Charlemagne to defend Christendom. As one chronicler put it, "Once we had a king, now we have kinglets." Or, as another said in 909: "Every man does what seems good in his own eyes, despising laws human and divine and the commands of the Church. The strong oppress the weak, the world is full of violence against the poor and of the plunder of ecclesiastical goods."[8] In the midst of the chaos, a system known generically as *feudalism* evolved to provide for economic livelihood and law and order at the grassroots level.

Medieval society divided people into two primary classes, the nobility and the serfs (or peasants). Only the nobility were involved in feudal politics. Both the nobility and the serfs were involved in the economic side of feudalism, known as *manorialism*. Both feudalism and manorialism were composed of a personal element, a property element, and a governmental element.

In feudalism, every man was a vassal, having sworn fealty (loyalty) to a lord. Each vassal owed his lord many obligations. The most important of these was military service as an armed, mounted knight for a customary thirty days per year. The lord owed his vassal many obligations in return, including protection and justice in the lord's court. This was the personal element. In

---

[8] Roland H. Bainton, *Christendom: A Short History of Christianity and Its Impact on Western Civilization, vol. 2, From the Birth of Christ to the Reformation* (New York: Harper & Row, 1966), 164.

order for the vassal to fulfill his economic obligations, his lord invested him with a grant of land, or fief. This was the property element. The vassal had responsibility to ensure law and order on his fief, the governmental element. In theory, there was a pyramid of lords and vassals, with the king, or emperor, at the peak. In practice, however, there was a confusion of lords and vassals with fiefs scattered, in some cases, throughout Europe. For example, in the twelfth century, the Count of Champagne was the vassal of nine different lords and was himself the lord of vassals, who were also the vassals of eighty other lords. The important point is that these relationships were between individuals, not between an individual and the state, kingdom, or other political unit.

Manorialism worked similarly. The serfs on a lord's manor surrendered their freedom to their lord. They became tied to the land they worked. The serfs owed their lord a portion of the land's produce, among other obligations. The lord of the manor owed his serfs protection and justice in the manorial court. Together, feudalism and manorialism provided a measure of stability in the absence of any central governmental authority.

With the fragmentation of the Carolingian empire into a feudal patchwork quilt, the papacy was left without a protector. The church became corrupted by feudalism. Priests, bishops, archbishops, abbots of monasteries, even the pope, became feudal appointees of secular lords. In a feudal society where wealth is measured by ownership of land and serfs, the medieval church, owning approximately one-third of all available land, was a great source of wealth. Many of those who occupied church offices had little, if any, interest in spiritual matters. Those who did were plagued by divided allegiances.

Once the papacy became caught up in political struggle, the church entered a rapid and dramatic moral decline that lasted until the middle of the eleventh century. Between 897 and 955, there were seventeen popes, one of which was poisoned and crushed to death by his enemies. When Stephen VI (896–897) ascended the papal throne in 896, he had the corpse of his rival,

Formosus, disinterred and tried before a synod over which he presided. Once convicted, Formosus's corpse was stripped of its vestments, mutilated, beheaded, and thrown into the Tiber River. In 897, Stephen VI was overthrown by his opponents and cast into prison.

Two rivals occupied the papal throne in 903. Both ended their brief careers in prison. From 904 until the reforms of Otto I, the papacy was controlled by an Italian family whose debauchery equaled that of the worst Roman emperors. Actual control of the papacy lay in the hands of three powerful women (Theodora and her two daughters, Morozia and Theodora), who passed the papal throne between their paramours and illegitimate children. The low point for the papacy came with the reign of John XII (955–964), who became pope at only eighteen years of age. His moral corruption was so absolute that it is little wonder that the period is known in church history as the papal pornocracy.

THE REVIVAL OF THE CHURCH

A number of factors came together to bring about a revival in the church during the period known as the High Middle Ages (c. 1050–1300). One was the emergence of a strong feudal monarchy in Germany, beginning when Otto, the Duke of Saxony, was crowned Otto I, the first Holy Roman Emperor. In 963, Otto I marched into Italy and convened a synod to try John XII, the pope who in 962 had crowned him. John XII was convicted, not surprisingly, and a layman was chosen to become Pope Leo VIII (963–965). For the next hundred years the Holy Roman emperors exerted influence on the choice of pope.

Equally important was the emergence of a powerful reform movement within the church itself. Its goal was to restore the church to the purity of the early church. Their understanding of the Scriptures and canon law led them to focus on freeing the church, and the papacy in particular, from secular control. Then the church could fulfill its spiritual mission to be the salt and light of the world.

This reform movement was centered at the monastery of Cluny in eastern France. Cluny was unique among monasteries in its founding and its organization. In 909 or 910, the Duke of Aquitaine granted a charter for its establishment at Cluny. The charter stipulated that the monastery was to govern itself and be free of all lay and ecclesiastical control. It was to be under the direct protection of the papacy. Given the sad state of affairs in Rome at the time, the monastery found itself independent. The order spread and more than eleven hundred new monasteries were founded by the beginning of the twelfth century. Each monastery was headed by a prior subject to the abbot of Cluny. Thus each monk in the order was a monk of Cluny.

The Cluniac reform called for an end to the corruption and immorality that had come to characterize the life of the church. The trafficking in church offices (simony) and the appointment of relatives to church offices (nepotism) were denounced and clerical celibacy enforced. Cultivation of the spiritual life and an emphasis on worship were encouraged.

The Cluniac reformers captured the papacy in 1073 with the election of one of their most outstanding monks, Hildebrand, as Pope Gregory VII (1073–1085). Hildebrand's path to the papacy began when Pope Leo IX (1049–1054), believing that a reformed clergy could lead and inspire the masses, chose Hildebrand as his chief advisor. Hildebrand became the power behind the papal throne.

Nicholas II (1059–1061) called the Lateran Council of 1059. With the aid of Hildebrand and Humbert, another Cluniac reformer recruited by Leo IX, Nicholas changed the manner in which future popes were chosen. The College of Cardinals was created to select a pope upon the death of the previous pope. Lay influence was eliminated as the choice of future popes came under control of the clergy.

With the election of Hildebrand as Pope Gregory VII in 1073, the stage was set for one of the most dramatic events of the Middle Ages—the showdown between Gregory VII and Henry IV (1056–1106). The excuse for the confrontation was the issue of lay investiture (see below). The real issue was the incompatibility of Gregory VII's vision of a papal monarchy and Henry IV's desire to retain control over the church in the Holy Roman Empire.

The practice of lay investiture involved a secular lord investing a bishop, abbot, or other churchman, with the insignia of his spiritual office. To Gregory VII, lay investiture symbolized lay authority over the church. He forbade any churchman from accepting a spiritual office from a lay ruler. Since Henry's rule in Germany depended upon his control of the church, he accused Gregory VII of being a false pope and called for a council to depose him. Gregory VII responded by excommunicating Henry IV and calling for a meeting of the German princes to elect a new emperor.

At Canossa in northern Italy, Henry IV humbled himself and asked Gregory VII to forgive him and receive him back into the church. Gregory did so, but Henry soon forgot his promises of good behavior. In 1080, when Gregory VII again excommunicated Henry IV, Henry invaded Italy and occupied Rome. Gregory was forced to flee to Sicily, where he died in exile. The question of lay investiture was eventually resolved in a compromise between Henry V (1086–1125) and Pope Callistus II (1119–1124). In the Concordat of Worms (1122) it was agreed that a churchman would swear loyalty to his secular, feudal lord, but the insignia of his spiritual office would be handed to him by the pope or one of his agents.

The zenith of papal power was reached during the pontificate of Innocent III (1198–1216). Innocent III claimed that the pope was truly the vicar of Christ on earth with the authority to rule not only the church but the whole world. All secular authority was derived from the pope, who was below God but above man. No individual came as close to achieving such exalted authority as did Innocent III. In the age of faith, Innocent possessed three powerful weapons in the publication of Gratian's *Decretum* (1140): a new definitive collection of canon law, the power to excommunicate, and the power to impose an interdict.

Excommunication cut the individual off from the church and its sacraments and denied the individual fellowship with other believers. In effect, the individual was damned. An interdict closed all the churches in a geographical area and forbade celebrating Mass and all other sacraments except for baptism of infants and extreme unction for the dying. The interdict was meant to cause such an uproar from the masses, who would fear for their salvation, that the stubborn king or emperor would have to submit.

In 1200, Innocent III placed France under an interdict to force Philip Augustus (1165–1223) to take back his lawful wife, whom he had attempted to divorce. In 1208, he placed England under an interdict, excommunicating King John in 1209, over John's refusal to accept Innocent's choice for archbishop of Canterbury. John was forced to surrender his kingdom to the pope and then receive it back as a fief, becoming a vassal of Innocent III. In 1212, Innocent imposed his will on the German princes when he determined the election of Frederick II as Holy Roman Emperor. In 1208, Innocent launched a crusade against southern France to wipe out the Albigensian heresy.

The Fourth Lateran Council, convened by Innocent III in 1215—one year before his death—was a fitting climax to his career. It clearly demonstrated the leadership of the church over Christendom at the beginning of the thirteenth century. A wide range of leaders from every level of church leadership (archbishops, bishops, abbots, friars, etc.) as well as secular lords were in attendance. The patriarch of the Maronite Christians, those Orthodox Christians in Syria who acknowledged the pope, was also present.

The council ruled on a wide range of subjects, from free education for the poor, to marriage vows, to matters touching on how God's grace was dispensed by the church for the salvation of souls. Among the better known of the seventy decrees issued were those that made annual confession and Mass attendance on Easter mandatory for every Christian. More importantly, transubstantiation, the teaching that in the Mass the bread and wine become the flesh and blood of Christ, was confirmed as official dogma. Thus the Mass became a sacrifice. On a darker note, the council issued decrees that would institutionalize religious anti-Semitism—a mind-set that lasted among Christians into the twentieth century. Jews were required to live in ghettos, not to appear in public during Holy Week, and (along with Muslims) to wear distinctive clothing.

It was not only the papacy that enjoyed a renaissance during the High Middle Ages. During the Middle Ages, when there was only one universal institutional church, spiritual revival often came in the form of the founding of new monastic orders. In 1097, the Cistercian order was founded at Citeaux in France. No one better exemplified the Cistercian vision of the Christian life as one of love and service than Bernard of Clairvaux (1090–1153). So persuasive were his sermons that mothers were said to have hid their sons, and wives, their husbands, when Bernard came fishing for souls. Even today, most Protestant hymnals include one or more hymns attributed to Bernard: "O Sacred Head Now Wounded," "Jesus, Thou Joy of Loving Hearts," and "Jesus, The Very Thought of Thee." Bernard led the defense of orthodox belief against those philosophers like Peter Abelard, who began to relativize truth.

Another order that sprung up during Innocent III's reign was the Order of Friars Minor, founded by Francis of Assisi. These Franciscans sought to call the church back to its first century roots, taking Christ as their example and devoting themselves single-mindedly to the service of the poor. Innocent III approved the order in 1209 and in 1212 authorized the founding of the Poor Claires, a sister order to the Franciscans. What a contrast between the figure of Innocent III in his robes of splender claiming lordship over all, and Francis of Assisi clothed in a ragged cloak with a rope taken from a scarecrow for a belt. Unlike Bernard and the Cistercians, Francis and his followers abandoned the monastery. They went out into the world preaching the gospel while ministering a cup of cold water in the Lord's name.

SCHISM, CRUSADES, AND SYNTHESIS
. . . .

The flowering of medieval civilization in Europe during the High Middle Ages meant that there were now two worlds, one with its axis in the East and the other with its axis in Europe. With the benefit of historical hindsight, we can perhaps see the split between East and West as unavoidable. The end of the barbarian invasions and success of feudalism made economic recovery possible, which in turn made possible the rise of feudal monarchies. At the same time, the papacy grew strong, able to assert its will over every area of life in Europe. These trends resulted in three major developments between the eleventh and the fourteenth centuries—the Great Schism, the Crusades, and the medieval synthesis (See chapter 4).

There were a number of reasons for the Great Schism of 1054 that split the Christian church into Roman Catholic and Eastern Orthodox. After 476, the pope became the *de facto* temporal and spiritual leader in the West. At the same time, the Eastern church fell under the control of the emperor in Constantinople. There was also a growing intellectual rift. The chaotic environment in the West compelled the Roman church to concentrate on issues of church government and organization, while the Eastern church, in a more stable environment, was free to debate abstract theological and philosophical issues.

There were, however, other more practical issues that illustrated the growing rift between East and West. Differences arose over clerical celibacy, the wearing of beards by priests, the use of Latin and Greek, the use of the *Filoque* clause in the Nicene Creed, and the date of Easter. Behind all of these issues was the papal claim to supremacy over the whole church. There would be no Synod of Whitby at which the Eastern Orthodox church would submit to papal authority as did the Celtic church in 664.

In 1054, the contested issue was the use of unleavened bread in the Eucharist by the church in the West. When Patriarch Michael Cerularius condemned the practice, the Byzantine emperor, hoping for reconciliation, invited Pope Leo IX to send a delegation to Constantinople. The papal emissaries included the Cluniac reformer, Cardinal Humbert. What was probably more a clash of personalities than anything else led to the dramatic events of July 16, 1054. Humbert and his colleagues placed a decree excommunicating the Patriarch and all his followers on the high altar of the Church of Saint Sophia. Cerularius responded by convening a synod that excommunicated the pope and all of his followers. In theory, all of Christianity was excommunicated and remained so until December 20, 1965, when Pope Paul VI (1963–1978) and Patriarch Athenagoras met and lifted the dual excommunications.

The split between Christians in the East and West was furthered by the Crusades. Launched in 1095 by Pope Urban II (1088–1099) and lasting until the last Crusader outpost in the Middle East fell in 1291, the Crusades were both a sign of progress in Europe and an expression of widespread popular piety. The movement was characterized by an emotionalism that emphasized Christ's suffering on the cross for the sins of humanity, the "cult of Mary" (viewing Mary as the compassionate intercessor between the penitent sinner and her Son), and the increased popularity of pilgrimages and saints' relics.

There was a mixture of motives behind the Crusades. Some Crusaders went for economic gain. Others simply sought adventure. For most, the Crusades were a pilgrimage. The eleventh and twelfth century chroniclers never speak of "Crusades" but of the "Jerusalem journey," the "journey to the Holy Sepulcher," or the "pilgrimage to Jerusalem." It was penance for a sinful life corrupted by a wicked world. For many, there was a longing to see the birthplace of God's Son, and perhaps to die there.

There were five "official" Crusades. The most successful was the first Crusade in 1096, which consisted largely of French nobility. After capturing Jerusalem on July 13, 1099, the Crusaders massacred the inhabitants. So many were slaughtered within Solomon's temple, that the floor was ankle-deep in blood. The massacre in Jerusalem and other atrocities committed by other Crusaders, including Richard I, the Lion Hearted, have hampered mission efforts among the Arabs ever since. Not all acts of barbarism were committed against Muslims, however. In 1204, the fourth Crusade attacked Constantinople. The fall of the city was followed by a frenzy of looting that some historians consider one of the greatest crimes of history.

The Crusaders established "Crusader Kingdoms" in the Middle East. The revival of trade between these kingdoms and Europe, especially after the fall of Constantinople, was one of the major influences of the Crusades. After 1097, the port cities of northern Italy began to flourish as a result. Along the trade routes from Italy to Flanders, towns began to reappear. There was also a revival of interest in classical learning, which led to the Renaissance of the fourteenth century.

TIMELINE FOR CHAPTER 3

496	Conversion of Clovis, King of the Franks
732	Charles Martel defeats Muslims at the Battle of Tours
756	Donation of Pepin creates future Papal States
782	Alcuin of York leads Charlemagne's palace school
800	Charlemagne crowned "Emperor of the Romans"
840	Charlemagne's Empire is divided between his three grandsons
840s	Height of Viking invasions
909/910	Monastery of Cluny founded
962	Otto I crowned first Holy Roman Emperor (Holy Roman Empire will last until 1806)
1054	Great Schism of West (Roman Catholic) and East (Greek Orthodox)
1095	Pope Urban II proclaims Crusades at Council of Clermont
1198-1216	Pope Innocent III, the height of papal power
1204	Fourth Crusade sacks Constantinople
1215	Fourth Lateran Council

CHAPTER FOUR

The Church under Siege:
The Late Middle Ages
and Renaissance

THE BIG PICTURE

The synthesis of faith and reason achieved during the High Middle Ages came under stress in the early fourteenth century and began to dissolve. Beginning around 1300 and continuing for the next two-and-a-half centuries, the effects of the Black Death, the Hundred Years' War, the decline of papal power, and the rise of a new secular worldview shattered the unity of faith and reason. The decline of papal power reached its nadir in 1309, when Clement V moved the papacy from Rome to Avignon in southern France. Having lost political power, the Avignon popes concentrated on perfecting an administrative structure to enrich its officeholders. Corruption, both financial and moral, became characteristic of the church hierarchy during the late Middle Ages. An attempt to curb the corruption by returning the papacy to Rome led to the existence of two popes, one in Avignon and one in Rome. At the height of the Great Schism of the Western Church (1378–1417), there were three rival popes. The schism was ended in 1417 by the Council of Constance. The new Renaissance popes divided their energies between regaining political control of the Papal States and assuming leadership of the cultural revival known as the Italian Renaissance. As the institutional church was increasingly distracted by Renaissance politics and culture, some began seeking a means of following Christ while ignoring, but not challenging, papal claims.

KEY EVENTS

1267–1273   The reconciliation of faith and reason by Thomas
            Aquinas in his *Summa Theologica* provides the
            intellectual basis for the Medieval Synthesis.

1309–1377   The unusually corrupt and worldly papacy of the
            Avignon era proves unable to provide spiritual
            comfort to a society suffering from plague and war.

1378–1417   The scandal of two and even three popes during the
            Great Schism of the Western Church seriously
            undermines the spiritual authority of the papacy in
            the eyes of the people.

1414–1418   The Council of Constance ends the schism but fails
            to reform the church.

1415   The burning of Jan Hus and Jerome of Prague by the
            Council of Constance dramatizes the inability of the
            church hierarchy to respond positively to those who
            demand reform.

On November 18, 1302, Pope Boniface VIII issued the papal bull
Unam Sanctam, perhaps the most forthright statement of papal
supremacy over kings. Boniface was locked in a bitter quarrel with
Philip IV (1268–1314) of France over Philip's arrest of a bishop.
Only six years earlier they clashed over Philip's taxing of the
French clergy. Boniface was forced to yield on the issue of taxation
but was determined not to do so again.

In *Unam Sanctam,* Boniface VIII claimed that God had
granted two swords, one spiritual and one temporal. Both
swords, Boniface declared, "are in the power of the church. . . .
The one is exercised for the church, the other by the church, the
one by the hand of the priest, the other by the hand of kings and
soldiers, though at the will and sufferance of the priest." Since
"the spiritual power excels any earthly one in dignity and nobility," the spiritual power sits in judgment over the earthly
power. The "supreme spiritual power [the pope] can be judged
only by God." *Unam Sanctam* concluded: "Therefore we
declare, state, define, and pronounce that it is altogether neces-

sary to salvation for every human creature to be subject to the Roman Pontiff."[9]

The papal bull was followed by a threat of excommunication. Philip IV decided to act first. On September 7, 1303, a band of Italian mercenaries, acting on orders from Philip, attacked the town of Anagni and took the elderly pontiff prisoner. Allies of the pope rallied the people and were able to free him. However, the shock and physical mistreatment that he suffered were too much for the old man. On October 12, 1303, Boniface died. The humiliation and defeat of Boniface VIII symbolizes the dissolution of the medieval synthesis during the fourteenth and fifteenth centuries, the period of the late Middle Ages.

Powerful economic, political, and intellectual forces were at work to undermine the universal rule of the church which characterized the High Middle Ages. The emergence of strong national monarchies in France and England challenged the exalted claims of papal supremacy voiced by Innocent III and Boniface VIII. The decline of papal power was accelerated by the schism, moral decline, and worldliness. Viewed against the backdrop of the Hundred Years' War and the Black Death, these scandals also undermined popular support for the church. A rebirth of interest in the classics in the middle of the fourteenth century threatened the unity of faith and reason achieved by the thirteenth-century scholastic theologians. Also the rise of individualism and the emphasis upon individual achievement shifted the focus from God to man as "the measure of all things." These momentous changes were reflected in the art, architecture, and literature of the period.

THE MEDIEVAL SYNTHESIS

The High Middle Ages were characterized by a rising population, revival of trade, growth of towns, and a powerful papal monarchy. The supreme achievement of the High Middle Ages,

[9] Brian Tierney, *The Middle Ages,* vol. 1, *Sources of Medieval History* (New York: Alfred A. Knopf, 1983), 315-316.

however, was the formation of a unified worldview that differed greatly from the classical (Greco-Roman) and modern worldviews. Based on Christianity, the medieval worldview gave meaning to history as well as to the individual. This synthesis, or unity, was achieved by reconciling reason and revelation. In the classical and modern worldviews, reason and revelation are at war with each other. If reason becomes autonomous, it displaces revelation as a source of truth. In the medieval synthesis, however, reason was able to explain and make understandable what was known by faith from revelation.

This synthesis of Christian revelation and Greek philosophy was the achievement of the scholastic philosophers, or "schoolmen." They were not seekers after truth. They sought to demonstrate through deductive logic what they already knew to be true by faith. Chief among the schoolmen was Thomas Aquinas (1225–1274), known as both the "Angelic Doctor" and the "Dumb Ox."

Aquinas's goal was to harmonize faith and reason, believing all truth comes from God, whether by reason or revelation. Aquinas believed that there was a body of truth that could be arrived at through reason and logic. Included was knowledge about the natural world, or science. Also included was knowledge about the existence of God and the immortality of the soul. For Aquinas, there was another body of truth that could be known only through faith. It included such doctrines as the Trinity, the Incarnation, original sin, and salvation. They did not contradict reason, for there could be no conflict between true faith and sound reason, both coming from God and together forming an organic whole. This unity was illustrated in Aquinas's two great literary works, the *Summa Theologica* and *Summa Contra Gentiles.* Intended to be a summation of Christian knowledge, the former is based on revelation, while the latter employs reason to support faith.

Aquinas's *Summa,* Dante's *Divine Comedy,* and the Gothic cathedral are the three great examples of the medieval synthesis. In the *Divine Comedy,* Dante takes the reader on a journey through hell, purgatory, and paradise. In so doing, he clearly portrays the medieval view of all creation as an orderly hierarchy.

The whole purpose of life is a pilgrimage to achieve salvation. What the *Divine Comedy* portrays in words and literary images, the Gothic cathedral portrays in stone. Gothic cathedrals, with their pointed arches, flying buttresses, soaring spires like hands outstretched to heaven, and large windows that bathe the interiors with light, testified to the medieval view of an orderly universe created by God.

According to the medieval synthesis, God was the reference point from which all creation derives its meaning. Apart from God's revelation, nothing could be understood. But as Aquinas demonstrated, God provided true knowledge through revelation and endowed human beings with the ability to understand it through reason. This worldview allowed human beings to live in a universe that made sense, a universe in which humanity felt at home.

DISSOLUTION OF THE MEDIEVAL SYNTHESIS

. . . .

At the beginning of the fourteenth century, the medieval synthesis came under stress and began to dissolve. The process continued for at least the next two hundred and fifty years. Indeed, some would argue that since the beginning of the thirteenth century, history has witnessed the gradual decline of the medieval synthesis. This stress came from the outbreak of the Black Death, the Hundred Years' War, the decline of the papacy, and the rise of a new, secular worldview—the Renaissance.

The fourteenth century in Europe opened with a severe economic downturn. Overpopulation caused a shortage of food. A silver shortage sparked spiraling inflation. Hard-pressed lords and poor knights turned to plunder and war. Crop failures resulted in famine. In some areas there were incidents of cannibalism. It was amidst these disasters that the Black Death struck Europe in 1347.

What has been called the Black Death (probably a combination of bubonic, pneumonic, and septicemic plagues) crossed Eurasia along the trade routes from Mongolia. It was carried by fleas on the backs of black rats. It first appeared in southern Europe in the shipping ports of Sicily and France in December 1347. By December 1349, it had crossed Europe and reached northern Scotland and southern Scandinavia. The first wave lasted until 1350, after which it surfaced periodically until finally disappearing from Europe in 1666. Between 19 and 38 million people died out of an estimated European population of only 75 million. In rural areas entire villages were wiped out. In some urban areas 50, 60, or even 80 percent of the population succumbed to the plague.

The impact of the plague upon an undernourished and unprepared population was devastating. In an age that knew nothing of bacteria or viruses, many explanations were given. An angel of death was said to visit the homes of plague victims. Jews were accused of poisoning the water supply, thus providing an excuse for frightened Gentiles to engage in massacres of their Jewish neighbors. The most scientific explanation came from the University of Paris, where it was suggested that an unusual alignment of the planets was causing the earth to give off a poisonous vapor.

The economic impact of losing roughly one-third of the overall population to the Black Death was significant. Labor shortages encouraged peasants to leave one manor for another or leave rural life altogether for the towns, where labor shortages were especially great. The impact on the church was likewise severe. The best clergy remained with their suffering parishioners, often dying with them. But those whose career in the church was a "living," rather than an opportunity to serve, simply fled at the first appearance of the plague. Those looking to the church for solace found a church racked by scandal at the highest levels.

DECLINE OF THE PAPACY

Upon the death of Boniface VIII in 1303, the College of Cardinals elected Benedict XI, who died the following year. In 1305 the cardinals elected a Frenchman, the Archbishop of Bordeaux, as Clem-

ent V (1305–1314). Clement established his residence at Avignon
in southern France. For the next seventy-two years, the popes, all of
whom were Frenchmen, were residents in Avignon. During the
"Avignon Captivity," or the "Babylonian Captivity of the Western
Church," the papacy was controlled by the French kings.

The papal court at Avignon was luxurious and opulent.
Francesco Petrarch, perhaps the greatest humanist scholar of the
time (and one of the church's severest critics), referred to it as "the
sewer of the world." The Avignon popes were great administrators
but poor spiritual leaders. Having lost political power, they concentrated on perfecting the church's legal system and financial organization. The church's administrative structure was designed to
enrich its officeholders while also providing funds for the French
monarchy, at war with England after 1337.

Always in need of additional revenues, the Avignon popes
resorted to the sale of indulgences and patronage. An indulgence
is a purchase of the remission of temporal punishment owed by a
repentant sinner for sins already forgiven. It is based on the teaching that the sinner is unable to do sufficient penance to merit full
forgiveness. Therefore, the sinner may draw from the Treasury of
Merits, a storehouse of the excess merits of Jesus Christ, the Virgin Mary, and the saints. Only the pope had the authority to with-
draw from the Treasury of Merits and apply them to a sinner's
account. The practice of granting indulgences in exchange for a
contribution to a church or monastery was not new. What was new
was the blatant selling of indulgences by the Avignon popes.

Patronage was another source of revenue exploited by the
Avignon popes. Certain offices (or benefices) in the church were
reserved for the papacy to fill. Eventually almost all major church
offices were papal appointments. To receive one of the offices, the
recipient had to pay a large tax to the papacy. In effect, church
offices were sold, often to the highest bidder. The system of
patronage led to other abuses. An individual might become the
holder of more than one church office, a practice known as pluralism, which was against canon law. Another particularly harmful
abuse to the pastoral work of the church was absenteeism, where

someone would receive the income from an office but never actually fill it. An Italian or Frenchman might be granted a benefice in England but never journey to England. He would receive the income from the office, while leaving the actual duties of the office to be fulfilled by some underpaid clerk.

As pressure mounted to return the papacy to Rome, Urban V (1362–1370) attempted to do so in 1367. Frustrated at his failure to bring peace to Italy and reunite the Roman and Eastern Orthodox churches, Urban moved back to Avignon in 1370. Upon his death later that year, Gregory XI (1370–1378) assumed the papal throne. Influenced by the Christian mystic, Catherine of Siena, Gregory returned to Rome in 1377, where he died in 1378. Yielding to public demand, the cardinals then elected an Italian, Urban VI (1378–1389). Urban proved too dictatorial for the cardinals, some of whom he tortured to death. The cardinals met, declared Urban's election void, and elected a new pope, Clement VII (1378–1394). Clement returned to Avignon, beginning the Great Schism of the Western Church, which lasted until 1417.

With two individuals claiming to be the successor of St. Peter, Christendom was in crisis. The scandal was particularly hard for the laity. The individual Christian was taught to believe that the church dispensed salvation through the sacraments. But what if the parish priest, from whom the individual received the sacraments, was ordained by a false pope? The link going back to St. Peter was broken. The individual's soul was in danger of eternal damnation, and there was nothing he or she could do about it. The authority of the church was further damaged as more people began to look for a way to bypass the church hierarchy and go directly to God.

The schism divided Christendom along political lines. France and her allies sided with the popes in Avignon. England, at war with France, naturally recognized the popes in Rome. Italy, the Holy Roman Empire, Scandinavia, and Hungary joined with England. In 1409, believing that a general council of the church was qualified to settle the schism, a group of cardinals called the Council of Pisa. Both popes were then deposed, and Alexander

V (1409–1410) was elected. The schism did not end. Where
there were two popes before, now there were three. The Council
of Pisa did succeed, however, in raising the crucial question of a
council having a power superior to that of the pope.

It was not only the church that was in confusion. In the years
around 1400, there were two claimants for the throne of England,
two aristocratic factions contending for control of France, and
three princes contending for the imperial crown of the Holy
Roman Empire. In the church, the solution was found in the
Conciliar Movement, which asserted that a general council was
superior to the pope and therefore possessed the authority to
determine who was the true pope.

On November 5, 1414, a general council of the church opened
under the authorities of Pope John XIII (1410–1415) and
Emperor Sigismund (1361–1437) in Constance, a city situated
on Lake Constance between Germany and Switzerland. The
council lasted until 1418. Its task was to achieve three things:
end the schism, combat heresy, and reform the church. It was
attended by over 350 high church officials, including representatives from the Greek Orthodox church.

On the positive side, the Council of Constance resolved the
schism. On May 29, 1415, John XIII was deposed and demoted to
the rank of cardinal bishop, following a trial in which the cardinals
accused him of seventy-two crimes. Gregory XII (1406–1415) of
the Roman line resigned. Benedict XIII (1394–1423) of the
Avignon line was deposed by the council in 1417. He refused to
accept the council's ruling and took up residence in Peniscola,
Spain, where he continued to believe he was the true pope until his
death. Having eliminated all three rivals, the council then elected
Martin V (1417–1431), who returned to Rome in 1420. Martin set
about rebuilding Rome and restoring order in the Papal States.
Spiritual issues were not a priority with him.

The schism was over, but the question of a general council's
authority to remove and elect popes was not settled. Efforts to
transform the papacy into a kind of constitutional monarchy continued until 1449, when the Council of Basel dispersed, having

admitted defeat. In 1460, Pope Pius II (1458–1464) issued a papal bull, *Execrabilis,* condemning any future appeals to a general council. Henceforth, any reform of the Roman Catholic church had to be initiated by the pope. But beginning with Eugene IV (1431–1439), the church entered upon the era of the Renaissance popes. The course was set that would ultimately lead to the outbreak of the Reformation in 1517.

With respect to the issues of reform and heresy, the council's actions were a mixture of apathy and tragedy. Committees were formed to work on ways of reforming the numerous abuses in the church. A bill of particulars was drafted and presented to Martin V, who chose to ignore it. Reform was tabled. As to heresy, Jan Hus (1373–1415) was summoned to Constance to explain his teachings. The safe conduct granted by Emperor Sigismund was withdrawn after Hus's arrival in Constance. Hus was charged with heresy, tried, convicted, and burned at the stake. His associate, Jerome of Prague (c. 1371–1416), was also burned at the stake. Since Hus's teachings were based upon those of the Oxford scholar John Wycliffe (c. 1320–1384), Wycliffe's books were burned and his body exhumed. In 1428, Wycliffe's bones were burned and the ashes thrown into the Swift River.

THE RENAISSANCE

Perhaps the most dramatic evidence of the dissolution of the medieval synthesis was the revival of interest in classical civilization and its values. This revival began in northern Italy in the middle of the fourteenth century and spread throughout western Europe during the following two centuries. It was the northern Italian cities (Milan, Florence, Genoa, and Venice) that led the way in the commercial revival that followed the Crusades. The struggle between the popes and the Holy Roman emperors left the city-states of northern Italy free to develop their own culture. By the early-fifteenth century, a lively urban culture existed that was centered at the princely courts of the despots and oligarchs that ruled the city-states.

The urban environment of the Italian cities promoted a secular spirit that emphasized individualism and individual achievement. The self-made man was the hero of the day. It was a very youthful culture. With life expectancy at only forty years for men (eighteen during the plague), leaders in business, politics, and the church were often under thirty-five years old. Their leadership displayed the characteristics of youth—impatience, imagination, quick recourse to violence, and a love of extravagance. Because commercial activity was the focus of urban life, there was a high level of literacy and interest in practical education.

The classical tradition had always been stronger in Italy than elsewhere in Europe. The fall of Constantinople to the Ottoman Turks in 1453 sent a flood of classical scholars and manuscripts to Italy. Scholars like Petrarch soon took a lively interest in the classical manuscripts, especially those in Latin. There they found a spirit akin to their own age. It was a spirit that focused upon this world and upon people and what they could achieve. Leon Battista Alberti summed it up well when he said, "Men can do all things if they will," echoing the ancient Greek philosopher Protagoras who said, "Man is the measure of all things." From the work of artists and sculptors, who portrayed biblical characters as real people in a real world rather than symbols of spiritual truths, to architects who built buildings scaled down to human proportions rather than soaring Gothic cathedrals, the new world of Renaissance culture was one in which people found meaning in their own achievements. Gone was the God-centered universe of the medieval synthesis where God was the axis that gave meaning to all of his creation.

Although the Renaissance in Italy was clearly secular in spirit, it was not secular to the same extent, north of the Alps. The humanist scholars in Italy—like Petrarch, Pico della Mirandola, Baldassare Castiglione, Niccolo Machiavelli, and Lorenzo Valla, to name only a few—were primarily interested in the classical authors and languages of ancient Greece and Rome. North of the Alps, humanist scholars like Desiderius Erasmus, Thomas More, John Colet, and John Reuchlin turned their interest to the writings of the early church. There they hoped to find a purer form of Christianity that could bring revival to the church of their own day. Whereas the Italian Lorenzo Valla used textual criticism to prove the *Donation of Constantine* was a forgery from the eighth century, Erasmus used his humanist linguistic skills to produce a new Greek translation of the New Testament. Each in his own way contributed to the coming of the sixteenth-century Reformation.

The Renaissance popes displayed the characteristics, both good and bad, of the Italian Renaissance. Many were great patrons of the arts. Most were very astute princes of the Papal States. Unfortunately, spiritual concerns were not a priority with them. Perhaps Leo X best expressed the attitude of the Renaissance popes, when he wrote to his brother shortly after becoming pope: "Let us enjoy the papacy, for God has given it to us."

Nicholas V (1447–1455) is considered the first Renaissance pope. He was a man of peace, well versed in theology, the Scriptures, and the literature of the early church. A devoted humanist, he founded the Vatican Library. He searched monastic libraries all over Europe for manuscripts and encouraged the translation of Greek manuscripts into Latin. In addition to the Vatican Library, Nicholas helped to found libraries in Florence, Urbino, and Pesaro. In 1453, he survived a plot by a Roman nobleman to assassinate him and the cardinals while at Mass in St. Peter's cathedral.

Nicholas V was succeeded by Callistus III (1455–1458), an able administrator who halted Nicholas's building projects and dismissed the humanists and artists from the papal court. During his brief reign (he was nearly eighty years old), Callistus freely dispensed honors, benefices, and high church offices to his dishonorable nephews. Callistus III was followed in 1458 by Pius II (1458–1464), also a generous patron of his family.

Pius II came from a family of eighteen children, though only he and two sisters survived the plague. As pope, Pius's chief goal was to regain firm control over the Papal States, a goal that kept him constantly at war. One of his enemies, the Lord of

Rimini, he canonized to hell. Pius II was followed by Paul II (1461–1471), a vain person who lived like a Renaissance prince.

Unlike his three predecessors, Sixtus IV (1471–1484) came from humble origins. He rose through the Franciscans to become general of the order in 1464. As pope, his nepotism brought the papacy to the point of bankruptcy. In 1478, he was implicated in a plot to assassinate the powerful Florentine banker and humanist, Lorenzo de Medici, and his brother while they attended Mass. When the plot failed, Sixtus IV excommunicated Lorenzo and placed Florence under an interdict. In that same year, Sixtus established the infamous Spanish Inquisition.

Riots broke out in the streets of Rome upon Sixtus's death. The papal election of 1484 that brought Innocent VIII (1484–1492) to the papal throne was a fraud. At that time, votes were simply purchased by the candidates, and Innocent outbid his rivals. When the general of the Augustinian order criticized Innocent by saying, "In darkness Innocent was elected, in darkness he lives, and in darkness he will die,"[10] he was thrown into prison. Rome became a refuge for criminals during Innocent's reign. Asked why the laws were not enforced, Rodrigo Borgia, Innocent's vice-chancellor, replied, "God desires not the death of a sinner, but rather that he should pay and live."[11] One Italian poet commented that Innocent *deserved* to be called "father," since he had sixteen illegitimate children, all by married women. Many of the cardinals mirrored Innocent's lifestyle, openly acknowledging their illegitimate children.

Of the cardinals who participated in the election of Rodrigo Borgia as Alexander VI in 1492, only five did not sell their votes. Alexander devoted his reign to furthering the careers of his illegitimate children, especially the notorious Cesare Borgia, who served as the model for Niccolo Machiavelli's ideal ruler in *The Prince*. A contemporary described Alexander VI as an impressive figure, who attracted women like a magnet attracts iron. Both Alexander

[10]Quoted in Philip Schaff, *History of the Christian Church,* vol. 5, pt. 2, *The Middle Ages* (New York: Charles Scribner's Sons, 1910), 437.
[11]Ibid.

and his son, Cesare, were poisoned by mistake when they took poison they had allegedly intended for a cardinal. When Cesare heard of his father's death, he sent a cardinal to obtain the keys to the papal treasury, although he was himself dying. The Duke of Mantua wrote to Alexander's daughter, the famous Lucrezia Borgia, that when Alexander lay dying, bloated and foaming at the mouth, seven demons were present in the room.

Following the brief, month-long pontificate of Pius III, Rodrigo Borgia's old rival, Julian Ravere, was elected Julius II (1503–1513). In 1492, Rodrigo had outbid Julian. In 1503, Julian was able to purchase sufficient votes to win the election. Julius II made strengthening the political authority of the papacy his chief goal. He employed Swiss mercenaries and often led his armies into battle while trying to drive the French out of Italy. Known to history as the "Warrior Pope" and in his own day as "Papa Terrible," Julius II is also particularly remembered for his patronage of the arts. He employed such famous Renaissance artists as Michelangelo, Raphael, and Bramante. It was during Julius II's reign that the two future Reformers, Martin Luther and Huldrich Zwingli, visited Rome.

Leo X (1513–1521), the last Renaissance pope, was Lorenzo de Medici's second son, Giovanni. In many ways Leo personified the ills that afflicted the Renaissance church. He perfected the arts of nepotism, pluralism, and absenteeism long before becoming pope. He took holy orders at age seven and was given the abbey of Fonte Dolce. At eight years of age, Leo was nominated for an archbishopric. Innocent VIII appointed him a cardinal-deacon when he was only fourteen. And at age seventeen, Leo became the youngest cardinal, ever. In all, he held nearly thirty church offices while still a teenager. Ironically, shortly before his death, Lorenzo wrote to Giovanni warning him that Rome was the sink of all iniquities and exhorting him to live a virtuous life.

During Leo X's reign, Rome became a center for the arts. Leo was a great patron of the arts and was determined to complete St. Peter's cathedral. It was in part the need to secure funding for St. Peter's that led Leo X to authorize the selling of indulgences in

Germany—a bit of poor judgment that eventually contributed to the Protestant Reformation.

Not all was bleak in the church during the late Middle Ages and Renaissance. The advancement of Christ's church does not depend upon human initiative. Even during the dark periods of church history, Christ continues to build his church. And so it was during the sad era just discussed. Though the church hierarchy was corrupt, individual believers remained true to the call of Christ. Some, like Jan Hus, or Girolamo Savonarola, a Florentine preacher who criticized Alexander VI's immorality, suffered martyrdom. The Lollards (followers of John Wycliffe) and the Waldensians (followers of Peter Waldo) were relentlessly persecuted during the fourteenth and fifteenth centuries. Many others avoided direct confrontation and martyrdom by simply joining the movement away from institutional to personal religion. Religious mysticism flourished during the period, especially in Germany. Some of the mystics, like Catherine of Siena, became very influential, even within the institutional church.

Still others sought to fulfill the command to take the gospel to all parts of the world. The two leading orders of friars, the Franciscans and Dominicans, were prominent in such efforts. Following the example of their founder, Francis of Assisi (who went to Egypt to preach the gospel to the Muslims), Franciscans went to North Africa. In Fez and Morocco, they established dioceses, but only temporarily. All across central Asia and the Far East, both Franciscans and Dominicans traveled as missionaries. Their hope was to convert the vast Mongol conquest before the Mongols converted to Islam.

The Mongols, whose native religion was a form of shamanism, were not hostile to the Christian missionaries. Nestorian Christians were already active among them. Genghis Khan (c. 1162–1227) married one of his sons to a Christian princess, who became the mother of Kublai Khan (1215–1294). Mangu, Grand Khan from

1251 to 1259, was said to have been baptized—although by an Armenian. In any case, the Mongol conquest threw the door open to Christian missions from Russia to China during the latter thirteenth and the fourteenth centuries. Soon Franciscans and Dominicans were competing with Muslim missionaries for souls in Persia, India, Samarkand, and China. Giovanni da Montecorvino arrived in Cambaluc (Beijing) in 1294. He established two churches, translated the New Testament and the Psalter, and was appointed archbishop in 1307.

These early mission efforts were short-lived. The church of the late Middle Ages and Renaissance was not able to support such efforts. When the Mongol Khan Uzbek, khan of the Golden Horde (southern Russia), converted to Islam, the lines of communication with the mission fields in eastern Asia were cut. Then in 1368, the Ming dynasty expelled all foreigners from China. Christian missions were forced to retreat from the Orient, until a new outburst of missionary activity was begun by the Jesuits in the wake of the Protestant Reformation.

TIMELINE FOR CHAPTER 4

1273	Thomas Aquinas writes *Summa Theologica*
1309–1377	Babylonian Captivity, Avignon papacy
1321	Dante Alighieri completes *Divine Comedy*
1337–1453	Hundred Years' War between England and France
1347–1351	Black Death ravages Europe
1378–1417	Great Schism of the Western Church
1384	Death of John Wycliffe
1414–1418	Council of Constance
1415	Martyrdom of Jan Hus
1453	Fall of Constantinople to Turks
1498	Martyrdom of Savonarola

CHAPTER FIVE

Back to the Bible:
The Protestant Reformation

THE BIG PICTURE

Martin Luther was not the first to call the church back to its first love. Others, such as the Waldensians, John Wycliffe, and Jan Hus, preached the same fundamental truths a hundred years or more before Luther. Still others, like Geert Groote and the Brethren of the Common Life, did not directly challenge the authority of the church hierarchy, but emphasized a direct personal relationship with Jesus Christ. The political interests of the new national monarchs, aided by the new intellectual climate provided by Christian humanists like Erasmus of Rotterdam, allowed the Reformation to occur with Luther at the beginning of the sixteenth century. Once launched, the Reformation soon fragmented into the "magisterial" Reformation and the "radical" Reformation. The former were the followers of Luther, Calvin, and Zwingli. The latter were a group of minor sects whose position on the separation of church and state, and the church as a body of believers, led to their persecution by both Catholic and Protestant authorities. A passion for truth characterized the Reformation. A common belief that conformity to accepted doctrinal truths was necessary to assure the salvation of the masses led to acts of persecution by both Catholics and Protestants. Religious tolerance began to make an appearance as monarchs like Elizabeth I put dynastic and state interests before religious conformity.

KEY EVENTS

1517	Luther posts his Ninety-five Theses, questioning the selling of indulgences and other church practices; launches the Protestant Reformation.
1534	The Society of Jesus (Jesuits), which eventually leads the Catholic offensive against Protestantism by emphasizing education and missions, is founded by Ignatius Loyola.
1536	John Calvin provides the first systematic definition of the new Protestant faith with the publication of his *Institutes of the Christian Religion*.
1545–1563	The Roman Catholic church responds to the Protestant Reformation by reaffirming the doctrine of the medieval church at the Council of Trent.
1563	The British Parliament passes the Thirty-Nine Articles, providing a model for religious peace that is followed by future pragmatic rulers who put the interests of state above religious conformity.

On the afternoon of April 16, 1521, Martin Luther (1483–1546), a monk of the Augustinian order, appeared before the Imperial Diet of the Holy Roman Empire, meeting in the city of Worms on the Rhine River. It was the first Diet presided over by Charles V (1500–1558), then only twenty-one years old. Luther's prince, the powerful duke of electoral Saxony, Frederick III, "the Wise" (1463–1525), only consented to Luther's appearance after assurances that Luther would not suffer the same fate as Jan Hus.

Luther's road to Worms had begun on October 31, 1517, when he nailed a list of ninety-five theses on the church door in Wittenberg, where he was serving as a professor at the university. Luther's ninety-five theses were an invitation to debate the sale of indulgences and other church practices. Written in Latin and intended only for other scholars at the university, these ninety-five theses were copied down, translated into German, and, thanks to the recently invented printing press, distributed throughout Germany. A combination of apathy and politics kept Pope Leo X from recognizing the threat represented by Luther's theses and from taking immediate and decisive measures to silence him.

In July 1519, Luther met and debated the wily Roman Catholic scholar, Johann Eck, in Leipzig. In the course of the debate, Eck was able to get Luther to admit that some of his views, especially as to the question of authority, were identical to those of Jan Hus, condemned as a heretic by the Council of Constance. Luther, in effect, admitted that he, too, was a heretic, as defined by the church. In June 1520, Leo X issued the papal bull *Exsurge Domine* condemning forty-one of Luther's teachings as heresy. Luther was given sixty days to recant or suffer excommunication. In January 1521, the final bull of excommunication against Luther was issued.

To Charles V, Luther represented a threat to the unity of the dynastic empire over which he ruled. The Hapsburg lands extended well beyond the Holy Roman Empire, and included much of eastern Europe, the Low Countries, Spain, and most of the "New World." The one thing that all his subjects had in common was their Roman Catholic religion. The possibility of a German national church, and perhaps a political union within Germany, threatened the very existence of the Hapsburg empire. Charles had to find a way to deal with Luther without provoking a civil war in Germany. Granting Luther a hearing before the Imperial Diet seemed to be the wisest solution. But Charles had no intentions of allowing Luther to continue disseminating his ideas.

Luther's appearance before the Diet on April 16, 1521, must have been dramatic. Luther was of peasant and lower middle-class background. At Worms, he stood alone in his monk's habit before the assembled ecclesiastical and lay lords of the empire, all decked out to show forth their rank and power. Luther came prepared to defend his writings. Instead, he was shown a stack of books and asked if he had written them. After responding in the affirmative, he was asked if he wished to retract the contents of any of them. Caught off guard, Luther asked for, and was granted, time to consider his response. On the afternoon of April 18, Luther again appeared before the Diet.

When the questions of the previous meeting were repeated, Luther began to explain the nature of his various writings. He was cut off and asked to give a simple answer to the question, "Do you wish to retract?" Luther's reply was brief, but it marked a watershed in the history of Christianity: "Unless I am convinced by the testimony of the Scriptures or by clear reason . . . I am bound by the Scriptures I have quoted, and my conscience is captive to the Word of God. I cannot and will not retract anything, since it is neither safe nor right to go against conscience." After a pause, he continued in German, "I cannot do otherwise; here I stand; may God help me."[12]

An extraordinary thing happened at Worms. An ordinary Christian stood up before the highest ecclesiastical and lay authorities of the day and refused to deny what he knew to be true, because it came from God's Word (revelation) and did not contradict reason. Here was a boldness based upon faith supported by reason. The Reformation was in the final analysis a debate over authority. It was not new. Authority has always been the key issue, ever since the serpent posed the question, "Did God really say . . ." (Genesis 3:1).

BACKGROUND

The question of why the Reformation occurred with Luther at the beginning of the sixteenth century, and not earlier, has always intrigued students of church history. To simply suggest that the church of Luther's day was riddled with corruption and ripe for destruction is unsatisfactory. As we have seen, there were earlier periods when the church leadership was more corrupt. To suggest that Luther was the first to go straight to the heart of the matter when he appealed to the authority of Scripture over that of the church is inaccurate. Likewise, Luther was not the first to "rediscover" the doctrine of salvation by grace through faith alone, or the doctrine that the individual may look directly to

[12]Quoted in R. Tudur Jones, *The Great Reformation* (Downers Grove, IL: Intervarsity Press, 1985), 44.

God (priesthood of the believer) for salvation and fellowship, rather than go through the institutional church. The development of the papal monarchy and the sacramental system obscured these truths but did not fully blot them out.

During the last quarter of the twelfth century, a merchant from Lyons, France, was converted after reading the New Testament. Peter Waldo (or Valdes) gave up his property and founded a group known as the "Poor Men," who went out as lay preachers. Excommunicated in 1184 and vigorously persecuted during the thirteenth century, the Waldensians survived and continue to exist as a small group in northern Italy. They rejected many practices and beliefs of the medieval church, such as purgatory, praying to the saints, and praying for the dead. In at least two key doctrines—the final authority of the Bible and the importance of making the Bible available in the language of the people—they anticipated Luther and the Reformation.

During the fourteenth century, John Wycliffe, sometimes called the "Morning Star of the Reformation," preached against transubstantiation and the belief that the church with its sacraments and priesthood was a necessary intermediary between the individual and God. Wycliffe took his stand on the authority of Scripture. Believing that the Bible was the authority for faith and practice, Wycliffe translated it into English. His followers, known as "Lollards," went out as lay preachers, spreading Wycliffe's teachings and preaching the gospel. Wycliffe's ideas were condemned in 1409 by church authorities in London, but Wycliffe enjoyed the protection of the powerful duke of Lancaster, John of Gaunt, and was allowed to retire. He died in his own bed in 1384. As noted earlier, the Council of Constance condemned Wycliffe's teachings as heresy.

During Wycliffe's tenure as a professor at Oxford, some students from Bohemia, among them Jerome of Prague, took copies of Wycliffe's writings back to Bohemia. There, the popular preacher of Bethlehem Chapel in Prague, Jan Hus, read Wycliffe's ideas and was highly influenced by them. Soon Hus was preaching against indulgences and appealing to the authority of Scripture. Hus's fate was sealed when Wenceslas IV (1361–1419), king of Bohemia, withdrew his support of Hus. As a result of a corrupt bargain between Wenceslas and his brother Sigismund, King of Hungary and Holy Roman Emperor, Hus was surrendered to the Council of Constance, where he was condemned and executed as a heretic. His ashes were thrown into the Rhine River.

A link exists between Wycliffe, Hus, and Luther, in that each preached the basic doctrines of the Reformation: the authority of Scripture and salvation by grace through faith in Jesus Christ. Also important for setting the stage for the Reformation was the movement known as *devotio moderna,* or modern devotion, a spiritual renewal movement that emphasized personal devotion and education. This movement was particularly strong in the Low Countries and western Germany. It had begun in the late fourteenth century and is usually associated with a Dutchman, Geert Groote (1340–1384).

Groote was a wealthy, worldly man who was converted in 1374 following a serious illness. After three years as a Carthusian monk, Groote took to preaching. Known for his piety, he also wrote tracts against the abuses within the church and the immorality of the clergy. His license to preach was withdrawn in 1383. Groote appealed to Rome but died of the plague before his appeal could be heard.

In 1380, Groote and his friends organized a group devoted to the cultivation of piety. Out of that group came the Brethren of the Common Life. The Brethren stressed piety and communion with God. They took a special interest in education. Soon they were found as teachers in many lay schools and even founded schools of their own. Their criticism of the church, their emphasis on educating the youth, and their stress on personal communion with God helped prepare the hearts and minds of many for the preaching of Luther and the other Reformers. Perhaps the best example of the influence of the Brethren of the Common Life is the book, *Imitation of Christ,* often cited as the best summation of their teaching.

Imitation of Christ is attributed to Thomas à Kempis (Thomas Haemerken, c. 1380–1471). The purpose of the book was to focus one's attention upon Christ and take Christ's example as the model for one's own life. "Many follow Jesus to the breaking of bread," wrote Thomas, "but few to the drinking of the cup of his passion. Many admire his miracles, but few follow him to the humiliation of his cross." Here was that radical commitment that has ever characterized the saints. "Poorest of all men," he concluded, "is he who lives without Jesus, and richest of all is he who stands in favor with Jesus." Over the intervening centuries since its first printing in 1471, the *Imitation of Christ* has appeared in thousands of editions, and remains one of the most popular Christian books ever written.

Desiderius Erasmus of Rotterdam (c. 1466–1536), perhaps the greatest of the Renaissance humanists, was educated in the Deventer School of the Brethren of the Common Life. Here was a link between the modern devotion, humanism, Christian humanism, and the Reformation. On a visit to England in 1499–1500, Erasmus was introduced to John Colet, Dean of St. Paul's Church, by his host, Sir Thomas More. From Colet, Erasmus learned the importance of knowing Greek. Erasmus spent the next three years in an intensive study of Greek. Between 1501 and 1516, Erasmus produced a string of books that have stood the test of time. Then in 1516, he published his greatest work and most important contribution to the Reformation, the *Greek New Testament.*

Erasmus's *Greek New Testament* was used by Luther following his condemnation by the Diet of Worms, when he spent almost a year translating the New Testament into German while in hiding at Frederick the Wise's Wartburg Castle. In his subsequent translation of the Old Testament and Apocrypha, Luther made use of other linguistic aids produced by the humanists, including Hebrew editions of Old Testament books as well as various grammars and glossaries. Some have suggested that Luther's translation would not have been possible without the earlier labors of humanist scholars.

There was, however, a fundamental difference between the Christian humanists, outspoken critics of the church though they were, and the Reformers. Christian humanism was based on the idea of human perfectibility. This was true of both the secular humanists of the Italian Renaissance and the Christian humanists of the Northern Renaissance. They believed, as did the ancient Greeks (and modern liberal Christians), that education could produce a moral person. The key to reforming the church was to remove corrupt individuals and replace them with morally upright men who would model their lives after the example of Christ. From the Christian humanists' vantage point, the doctrine of the church was sound. Such a view, of course, overlooked the effects of the Fall (see Genesis 3:1-24). Luther and the sixteenth-century Reformers insisted that as a result of the Fall, human nature was utterly depraved and could only be reformed by the grace of God.

This renewed emphasis on the true nature of fallen humanity is perhaps one of the most important contributions of the Reformation. The Reformers were led to the logical conclusion that it was corrupt doctrine, not simply corrupt men, that was the cause of the corruption in the church. Erasmus came to recognize this fundamental difference. At first, he defended Luther. When asked by Charles V what were Luther's chief errors, Erasmus replied that they were, "Two: he attacked the pope in his crown and the monks in their bellies."[13] But later, as Erasmus came to understand what Luther was really saying, he came out against Luther in his book, *On Free Will* (1524), in which he defended the idea that human effort contributes to one's sanctification and salvation. Luther countered with *On the Bondage of the Will* (1525), an appeal to the biblical teaching that, apart from God's grace, the individual can do nothing worthy of God's notice. Perhaps this fundamental difference is why no humanist of international reputation other than Luther's colleague at the University

---

[13]Quoted in Peter J. Klassen, *Europe in the Reformation* (Englewood Cliffs: Prentice-Hall, Inc., 1979), 49.

of Wittenburg, Philip Melanchthon (1497–1560), joined the
Protestant Reformation.

PROTESTANT REFORMATION
. . . .

The Reformation shattered the religious unity of Western Christendom forever. All of the Protestant churches that emerged from
the Reformation subscribed to the authority of the Bible and defended their doctrinal distinctives with appeals to Scripture.
They may be distinguished by the extent to which they departed
from the medieval Roman Catholic church, or the extent to
which they compromised with the political, economic, and social
realities of the time. In general, those which departed least from
the medieval church and compromised most with the political,
economic and social realities of the period are called the "magisterial" Reformation. Those that made the most radical break with
the beliefs and practices of the medieval church and tried hardest
to recreate the New Testament church are referred to as the "radical" Reformation.

The magisterial Reformation consisted of those churches that
followed the teachings of Luther, Calvin, and Zwingli and the
Anglican church in England. All abandoned the sacramental system of the medieval church and embraced the biblical doctrine of
salvation by grace through faith. They all continued the practice
of a territorial church, which fit well with the emergence of the
territorial nation-states. More than once, the Reformation spread
because the prince of a territory wanted a "national" church that
he could control and which would foster a sense of national identity. Whether Lutheran, Calvinist (Reformed, Presbyterian), or
Anglican, everyone within a given territory had to be of one
faith. The principle *cius regio eius religio,* of allowing each
prince to determine the religious faith of those living within his
territory, was the desired norm.

The continuance of the territorial church had certain logical
consequences. It was difficult, if not impossible, for most people
during the sixteenth and seventeenth centuries to believe that a

nation could be united if its citizens were of different religious faiths. Both Protestants and Roman Catholics believed that the individual must follow the religion of the state. Those who would not had to leave the territory or face the possibility of death. Apart from the radical Reformation, no church of the period believed in religious freedom. Catholics persecuted Protestants, Protestants persecuted Catholics and other Protestants, and both inflicted unspeakable horrors upon the followers of the radical Reformation. Religious tolerance, or freedom of religion, would be a by-product of the rise of secularism during the Enlightenment, not the Reformation.

The radical Reformation consisted of a diverse group of minor sects that had certain beliefs or practices in common—beliefs that set them apart from the magisterial churches. Among these was the belief in a believers' church, or a "gathered out" church. Only those who had made a confession of faith and were subsequently baptized were to be admitted to membership in the church. They desired not simply a reform of the church but wanted to restore the church of the New Testament as they understood it. This led logically to a separation of church and state and belief in religious freedom, both of which were seen as a threat to the emerging nation-states. Also, it led to a restoration of believer's baptism, or the practice of baptizing only those who have made a confession of faith. Just as a believer's church implied believer's baptism, the territorial church implied infant baptism.

Infant baptism was common by the end of the second century. Its practice grew along with the doctrine of original sin, for it was believed that baptism washed away original sin. Among the church fathers, Tertullian opposed it. By the late-fourth century, it was the norm in the West where it fit well with the medieval notion of Christendom. At first, the Swiss Reformer, Huldrich Zwingli, did not believe that there was any biblical basis for baptizing infants. Zwingli later accepted the practice when he discovered that believer's baptism would have the effect of depriving Christian citizens of Zurich of their franchise. Luther's colleague and successor, Philip Melanchthon, also questioned the biblical basis of infant baptism, but retreated when faced with the political implications of believer's baptism. Zwingli especially, but also Luther and Calvin and the Anglicans, envisioned a close collaboration between the reformed church and the state. Thus, it might be suggested that the practice of infant baptism was continued by the magisterial churches as a compromise with political reality. Subsequently, theological arguments developed to defend the practice.

The radicals' rejection of infant baptism as unscriptural and their return to a baptism of believers earned for them the name "Anabaptists," meaning "rebaptizers." Since rebaptism was a capital offense going back to the fifth century, their enemies, both Catholic and Protestant, had a convenient legal basis for persecuting and executing them. But it was more than the practice of believer's baptism that brought down upon them such wrath. Because of their belief in a life of discipleship—in which the individual Christian's relationship with Jesus Christ was more than an inner religious experience or an outward acceptance of doctrine—they were perceived as social, economic, political, and religious rebels. The true disciple of Christ would be distinguished by a wholly transformed lifestyle. For many, this meant a sharing of material goods, an embrace of pacifism, and a refusal to take oaths or serve the state.

Although the Reformation was a return to the authority of Scripture, and all Reformers, both magisterial and radical, agreed on that fundamental truth, there would not be any unified Protestant movement. Agreement on the authority of the Bible is not the same as agreeing on what the Bible says. The doctrine of the priesthood of believers guaranteed that fragmentation would characterize the history of the Protestant movement. The Reformers might agree on the Bible alone, grace alone, and faith alone but disagree passionately on the meaning of Communion, church polity, forms of worship, and many other issues.

Luther returned to Wittenberg from Wartburg Castle in 1522 to find the church in turmoil. Luther's colleague, Andreas von

Karlstadt, had made changes in the Mass and reordered church life (e.g., destroying images) that Luther had not sanctioned. Also, three individuals whom Luther dubbed the "Zwickau Prophets" appeared in Wittenberg preaching a doctrine that apparently placed immediate revelation from the Holy Spirit to the believer above the authority of the Bible. This was a dangerous doctrine that appeared also among some of the radical Reformers. Luther recognized that such radicalism would endanger the Reformation by bringing opposition from the princes. Luther had Frederick the Wise banish Karlstadt from Saxony. The Zwickau Prophets also found it advisable to leave.

Luther abhorred revolution and was committed to defending order in both the church and society. From June 1524 to July 1525, the peasants in Germany rose up in rebellion. Luther recognized that it was desperation that caused them to rebel. But when the peasants tried to justify their actions with an appeal to Scripture and Luther's teachings, Luther feared that their "radicalism" would unite the German princes against the Reformation. He called upon the princes to suppress the rebellion, which they did with unusual cruelty. The peasants felt betrayed, and many returned to Catholicism. After 1525, Lutheranism spread only to those areas where it was imposed by the state, as in the Scandinavian countries.

Luther rejected the idea of free church (*Freiwilligkeitskirche*), or voluntary fellowship of believers, as impractical. Giving up the idea of a believer's church meant also giving up believer's baptism. "If from now on only adults and older people were to be baptized," wrote Luther, "I venture to assert that not more than a tenth of our people would allow themselves to be baptized."[14] Luther taught that baptism was a sacrament and required faith in order to be valid. Thus Luther believed that infants had faith. If it could not be proven that infants had faith of their own, said Luther, then infant baptism should be aban-

---

[14]Quoted in William R. Estep, *Renaissance and Reformation* (Grand Rapids: William B. Eerdmans Publishing Company, 1986), 157.

doned at once, rather than "blaspheme the adorable majesty of God by such nonsensical and magical work."[15]

Generally, the Reformers reduced the sacraments to only two, baptism and Communion (the Lord's Supper). As with baptism, differences on Communion prevented unity. As the threat of a religious civil war within the Holy Roman Empire grew, Landgrave Philip of Hesse tried to bring the followers of Luther and Zwingli together. In the fall of 1529, Luther and Zwingli met at Philip's Marburg Castle to discuss their differences. Agreements were reached on many issues in this so-called Marburg Colloquy, but an impasse was reached on the question of Christ's presence in the Communion.

All the Reformers rejected the Roman Catholic doctrine of transubstantiation, whereby the bread and wine become the very body and blood of Jesus Christ—making the Eucharist a sacrifice. To them, transubstantiation appeared to deny Christ's words on the cross, "It is finished" (John 19:30). Luther, quoting Christ's words, "This is my body. . . . This is my blood" (Matthew 26:26, 28), believed that there was a real physical presence of Christ in the elements, though they remained bread and wine. Zwingli believed that Christ was spiritually present, but that Communion was simply a memorial service. He cited Christ's words, "Do this in remembrance of me" (Luke 22:19). John Calvin (1509–1564), the Geneva Reformer, took a position between Luther and Zwingli. He rejected the physical presence of Christ in the elements, but also rejected the notion that Communion was merely a memorial service. Instead, Calvin taught that Christ was spiritually present and "truly and effectually" received by the participant.

Zwingli was a Swiss patriot as well as a religious reformer. He desired a reform of society as well as the church. Also, Zwingli worked closely with the governmental authorities. The thirteen Swiss cantons had representative governments, and Zwingli believed that the Reformation should be instituted by those representative governments. His method was to engage in public

---

[15]Quoted in ibid., 158.

debates with representatives of the Roman Catholic church, after which the governmental authorities would introduce the Reformation. Zwingli was killed at the Battle of Kappel in 1531. In 1549, the Zwinglians merged with the Calvinists through the Consensus of Zurich. As noted earlier, the radical Reformation grew out of Zwingli's following.

COMPARISON OF 16TH-CENTURY CHRISTIAN TEACHING

	Roman Catholicism	Mainline Reformation	Radical Reformation
Basis of Authority	Bible plus Church Tradition	Bibles Only	Bible plus Inner Voice
Baptism	Infant Regeneration	Infant	Believers
Church	Universal	Territorial	Gathered Out
Church-State Relations	State submits to Church	State establishes Church	State and church are exclusive, hostile communities

John Calvin's great contribution to the Reformation was to provide the first systematic Protestant theology. Calvin came from a prosperous family. His father secured the income from a church benefice to pay for young Calvin's education. Calvin encountered Luther's ideas while a student at the University of Paris. After receiving the degree of Master of Arts in 1528, Calvin went on to study law at the universities of Orleans and Bourges, receiving his law degree in 1532. Calvin was converted sometime during 1532 or 1533. It was nothing so dramatic as Luther's conversion. In his only recorded reference to his conversion, Calvin says only that "by an unexpected conversion [God] tamed to teachableness a mind too stubborn for its years."[16]

[16]Quoted in ibid., 225.

In 1536, when Calvin was only twenty-seven years old, he published the first edition of the *Institutes of the Christian Religion.* The eighth and final revised edition appeared in 1559, five years before his death. Within the framework of Augustine's theology, the *Institutes* presented a clear, reasoned summation of Reformation theology. The influences of Luther and Zwingli, Erasmus's Christian humanism, and mysticism are evident. Calvin's theology is often summarized, and perhaps oversimplified, by the acronym TULIP: Total depravity, Unconditional election, Limited atonement, Irresistible grace, and Perseverance of the saints.

Apart from a brief period of exile in Strasbourg between 1538 and 1541, Calvin spent the years from 1536 to his death in 1564 in Geneva. Although Calvin never held an elected office in the government of Geneva, and at times found himself at odds with those who did, he nonetheless greatly influenced the government. Geneva under Calvin's influence was the closest Protestantism has ever come to having a Rome, and Calvin the closest thing to a Protestant "pope." Religious refugees from all over Europe went to Geneva to study under Calvin at the university he founded. Among the "Marian Exiles," those Protestants who fled England during the reign of Mary Tudor, was John Knox (c. 1514–1572), who introduced the Reformation to Scotland. Knox was so impressed with Calvin that he referred to him as "that noble servant of God," and Geneva under Calvin as "the most perfect school of Christ that ever was in the earth since the days of the Apostles."[17] From Geneva, numerous Calvinist missionaries like Knox went out to all parts of Europe, carrying the light of the Reformation.

Not everyone, however, found Geneva as congenial as Knox, nor were all religious refugees as welcomed. In 1542, the *Ecclesiastical Ordinances* were promulgated at Calvin's request. Among other things, it set up the Consistory to oversee the theological and moral life of the community. Wayward individuals could be punished with excommunication. When necessary,

---

[17]Quoted in Earle E. Cairns, *Christianity through the Centuries: A History of the Christian Church,* rev. 3rd ed. (Grand Rapids: Zondervan Publishing House, 1996), 313; Jones, 134.

more severe punishments were administered by the state. Within the next four years, fifty-eight people were executed and another seventy-six exiled. In one dramatic case, the anti-Trinitarian Michael Servetus, under a death sentence by the Inquisition in France, was burned at the stake. In another celebrated case, Jacques Gruet, a citizen who complained of Calvin's influence in a letter to the city officials, was arrested, tortured, and beheaded. Anabaptist refugees were not welcome in Geneva, either. In fact, in a letter to Henry VIII of England, Calvin urged Henry to burn Anabaptists as an example, for "it is far better that two or three be burned than thousands perish in Hell."[18]

The Protestant Reformers believed just as passionately in the truth as they perceived it as did Roman Catholics. Mary Tudor martyred over 275 Protestants in her attempt to return England to the Roman Catholic faith. She believed that by having left the Catholic church, her subjects had cut themselves off from the means of salvation. Horrible crimes were committed by both Catholics and Protestants under the mistaken notion that they were necessary to save multitudes from errors of belief that would lead to their eternal damnation.

The Reformation in England differed from that on the continent. It was passion of a different sort that led Henry VIII (1491–1547) to sever the ties between the church in England and Rome. Henry feared that should he die without a male heir, the War of the Roses would resume in England. He and his legitimate wife, Catherine of Aragon, had only one surviving child, Mary. Henry became convinced that God was punishing him for marrying his brother's widow, something forbidden by canon law based upon Leviticus 20:21. The solution appeared simple—divorce Catherine and marry the pretty Anne Boleyn, with whom he had fallen in love.

When negotiations with Pope Clement VII (1478–1534) broke down, Henry VIII decided to act through Parliament. In 1531, Henry forced the English clergy to accept him as the head of the church in England, "as far as the law of Christ allows." In 1532,

[18]Quoted in Estep, 241.

he appointed Thomas Cranmer (1489–1556) Archbishop of Canterbury. Cranmer convened a church court in 1533 that promptly granted the divorce. The following year, Parliament passed the Act of Supremacy, declaring Henry to be the "only supreme head" of the Church of England. The English church was now a national church, but it was not Protestant.

Henry VIII remained a Roman Catholic believer. He had even been granted the title "Defender of the Faith" by Pope Leo X for his pamphlet defending the seven sacraments against Luther's attack in *The Babylonian Captivity of the Church* (1521). In 1539, he had Parliament pass the Six Acts, which affirmed Roman Catholic theology. So long as Henry remained alive, only the head of the Church of England was different. It remained Roman Catholic in doctrine.

Henry VIII died in 1547 and was succeeded by his nine-year-old son, Edward VI (1537–1553). It was during the reign of Edward VI that the Protestant Reformation came to England. This was largely the work of Thomas Cranmer and two bishops, Nicholas Ridley and Hugh Latimer, all three of whom were eventually martyred during the reign of Edward's sister, Mary Tudor (1515–1568). Cranmer wrote the *Book of Common Prayer* in 1549 to provide a Protestant liturgy. In preparing a second edition (issued in 1552), and in writing a creed, the Forty-two Articles, Cranmer sought the advice of John Knox and other Calvinists who served as professors at the universities of Oxford and Cambridge.

Edward VI's early death in 1553 was a setback for the Reformation in England. A conspiracy to bypass the legitimate heir, Mary Tudor, in favor of her cousin, Lady Jane Grey, failed. The conspirators were arrested and executed, as was the unfortunate sixteen-year-old Jane Grey, who had been a mere pawn of ambitious men.

In October 1553, Parliament restored Henry VIII's marriage to Catherine and repealed all of the religious reforms enacted under Edward VI. Cranmer was replaced as Archbishop of Canterbury by Cardinal Reginald Pole, a member of the Oratory of Divine

Love and a leader of the Catholic Reformation. Pole became
Mary's closest advisor. At first, Mary left everyone free to follow
their own conscience, naively believing that the English would
return to the Catholic church. When they did not, she decided to
use force. In 1555, the burning of heretics began, earning for her
the epithet "Bloody Mary" in Protestant memory. Interestingly,
her sister and successor, Elizabeth I (1533–1603), martyred many
more people than Mary, yet is remembered as "Good Queen
Bess." Sadly, history is not always fair.

It was not Mary's overzealous attempt to restore Catholicism
that alienated her from her subjects so much as her marriage to
King Philip II (1527–1598) of Spain. She began her reign with
great popular support. Had she been willing to avoid religious
fanaticism, been content with restoring the Church of England to
where her father had left it, and listened to her subjects' wishes
and not married Philip II, her reign would likely have been a
happy one. Instead, like so many of the leaders of the Reformation era, she believed passionately in the truth as she understood
it. It remained for Elizabeth I, who cared little about religion
except as it affected the well-being of her realm, to bring religious peace to England.

Elizabeth was twenty-five years old when she became Queen
of England on November 17, 1558. Her religious settlement,
which took a moderate course, made her very popular with the
vast majority of her subjects. She took the title "supreme governor" of the Church of England, rather than the potentially offensive "supreme head." Cranmer's *Book of Common Prayer* of
1552 was adopted with minor changes. The Forty-two Articles
were adopted, also with minor revisions, until the Thirty-nine
Articles were passed by Parliament in 1563. In various ways,
moderate Catholics were made comfortable in Elizabethan England. Catholics could avoid mandatory, monthly attendance at
church by paying a token fine. Catholics could celebrate Mass in
private without fear of government interference—unless treason
was suspected. The words in the service of Holy Communion
were vague enough that they could be interpreted as either

accepting or rejecting transubstantiation. Trouble, however, came from passionate Calvinists, who wanted to rid the church of all remnants of "popery." It also came from passionate Catholics, encouraged after 1580 by the Jesuits, who sought Elizabeth's removal and a full restoration of Roman Catholicism. Most of her subjects, however, both Protestant and Catholic, welcomed Elizabeth's settlement. She remained popular throughout her reign.

With the Reformation, the universal church of the Middle Ages was replaced by national churches. Only the churches that came out of the radical Reformation opposed the union of church and state. Despite the numerous and ever-increasing distinctives that separated Protestants, they were united in their acceptance of the historic doctrines of the Christian faith: salvation by grace through faith, the sole authority of the Bible, and the priesthood of believers. The priesthood of believers also meant restoration of the individual's direct access to God. No longer was there any other intermediary needed except Jesus Christ.

Still, there remained certain truths held in common by both Protestants and Catholics. Among these were the historic creeds hammered out during the fourth and fifth centuries, the Trinity, the deity and resurrection of Jesus Christ, the Bible as God's revealed Word, a historic Fall, original sin, and a morally regenerated life for the believer.

The Reformation also led to the promotion of education. Both the Protestant Reformers and the Reformed Catholic church (See chapter 6) emphasized education. For the Protestants, who emphasized the authority of the Bible, it was necessary for the believer to be able to read God's written Word. The rise of empirical science in the Scientific Revolution after 1543 and the struggle for constitutional government may also be understood as being stimulated by the Reformation.

TIMELINE FOR CHAPTER 5

1517	Luther's Ninety-five Theses
1519	Leipzig debate

1521	Luther before the Diet of Worms
1523	Reformation in Zurich
1524–1526	Peasants' revolt in Germany
1525	First Anabaptist congregation
1527	Schleitheim Confession (Anabaptist)
1529	Lutheran princes protest at Diet of Speyer
	Marburg Colloquy
	Beginning of Reformation Parliament in England
1530	Augsburg Confession
1531	Death of Zwingli
1534	Ignatius Loyola founds the Society of Jesus (Jesuits)
1536	Publication of Calvin's *Institutes of the Christian Religion*
1538	Reformation established in Geneva
1545–1563	Council of Trent
1546	Death of Martin Luther
1547–1553	Edward VI, King of England
1553–1558	Elizabeth I, Queen of England
1555	Peace of Augsburg recognizes *cuius regio eius religio* principle
1556	Martyrdom of Thomas Cranmer, Nicholas Ridley, and Hugh Latimer
	Death of Ignatius Loyola
1563	Thirty-Nine Articles
1564	Death of John Calvin
1572	Death of John Knox

CHAPTER SIX

Orthodoxy and Passion: The Church in a Changing World

THE BIG PICTURE

The Protestant Reformation was followed by a century during which the Protestant churches developed their particular theologies while becoming established churches. The Catholic church, newly empowered by the Council of Trent, went on the offensive against Protestantism in Europe, launching the first great foreign missions movement. As with the Protestant churches, the growth of strong central governments meant that the Catholic churches, too, became established national churches.

Conservatives triumphed in both Protestantism and Catholicism. Among the Catholics, those like Cardinal Gasparo Contarini, who sought accommodation with the Protestant Reformation, lost to the conservatives who advocated combating and repressing Protestantism. The "liberals" found an outlet in foreign missions to the newly discovered "New World." In the Protestant camp, Jacobus Arminius tried to modify the strict double predestination of Theodore Beza, Calvin's successor, by allowing for the freedom of each individual as the image-bearer of God. A synod of Reformed churches meeting in Dordrecht, Holland, in 1618–1619 condemned Arminius's teachings. The Arminians found refuge in the emerging Pietist movement, and, like the Catholic reformers, in Protestant foreign missions.

KEY EVENTS

1541   The agreements reached at the Colloquy of
              Regensburg are rejected by both Catholics and
              Protestants, dooming the last hope for reconciliation.

1542–1552 Francis Xavier (a Jesuit) goes to Asia, launching the
              first foreign missions movement of later Christianity.

1618–1619 The Synod of Dordrecht defines orthodoxy for the
              Reformed faith, giving rise to the Calvinist-Arminian
              split among Protestants.

1688   The Glorious Revolution in England establishes a
              constitutional government and religious liberty for all
              but Catholics, Unitarians, and Jews.

By the 1560s, the Protestant Reformation had run its course, and
the Catholic Reformation had produced a revitalized Roman Catholic church now on the offensive against Protestantism. The new
Protestant churches were taken captive by the unreformed society
in which they existed and were thus spiritually unprepared to face
the challenges presented by the new political and economic forces
that were transforming Europe. The new absolutist governments on
the continent asserted control over the churches (both Protestant
and Catholic), transforming them into pillars of the existing order
rather than leaving them free to become the conscience of the new
nation-states.

The Protestant Reformation seems to have lost its drive by the
late-sixteenth century. Having established their independence,
Protestants settled down to a century or more of internal disputes
over doctrine. The followers of Calvin debated the meaning of
predestination and eventually split into "orthodox" and "Arminian." Lutherans split into "true (or 'strict') Lutherans" and
"Philippists" over whether too many concessions were being
made to Catholicism. Lutherans and Calvinists disagreed over
the Lord's Supper, the definitions of evil and sin, and what was
permissible in worship. A positive result of this preoccupation
with refining doctrine was the formation of Protestant creeds, but
the seventeenth century came to be known as the "century of
dead orthodoxy" for Protestantism.

PROTESTANT ORTHODOXY

The seventeenth century was the great century of Protestant scholasticism. Post-Reformation theologians did for Protestant theology what the thirteenth-century Schoolmen did for the Catholic church. Great systematic thinkers debated and refined Protestant doctrine in massive, multi-volume, carefully constructed, logical arguments that would have impressed, though not pleased, Thomas Aquinas and other scholastic theologians of the High Middle Ages. These Lutheran and Calvinist doctors of theology drew upon Aristotle's philosophy and logic to help them craft their ideas. Their goal was to provide a unified field of knowledge based upon an understanding of God and his creation as revealed in his infallible Scriptures.

Among the Lutherans, Johann Gerhard (1582–1637), Abraham Calov (1612–1686), and Johann Quenstadt (1617–1688) stand out. Johann Heinrich Alsted (1588–1638), Gisbert Voetius (1588–1676), and François Turretin (1623–1687) carried the banners for the Reformed tradition. There was agreement on the fundamentals of the faith, but differences on the particulars. Lutherans accepted predestination, but not the double predestination believed in by many of the Reformed faith. Even among Calvinists there was not full agreement on double predestination.

Perhaps the most significant doctrinal dispute among the Protestant thinkers involved Jacobus Arminius (1560–1609). Arminius questioned the strict double predestination as defined by John Calvin's successor, Theodore Beza (1519–1605). Arminius feared that strict double predestination runs the risk of making God the author of evil and denies individuals the freedom they possess as people created in God's image. A synod was held at Dordrecht (or Dordt), Holland in 1618–1619 to which all Reformed churches in Europe were invited. The Synod of Dordt rejected Arminius's teaching and defined orthodox Calvinism as essentially the opposite of Arminius's five points.

COMPARISON:
Five Points of Calvinism *vs* Five Points of Arminianism

Calvinism (Reformed)	*Arminianism*
T: Total depravity.	Individual capable of cooperating in salvation.
U: Unconditional election.	Election conditional on individual's choice.
L: Limited atonement.	General atonement.
I: Irresistible grace.	Grace can be resisted.
P: Perseverance of the saints.	Grace can be lost.

The outcome of the Synod of Dordt proved that even in Holland, the most tolerant nation in Europe at the time, tolerance had its limits. Many prominent political and intellectual leaders took sides in the controversy. The "orthodox" party held political power following the synod and used religion as an excuse to purge the world of their political opponents. Thus, the noted statesman Jan van Oldenbarneveldt, a supporter of Arminius, was executed on a charge of subverting religion. Others were imprisoned or forced to flee Holland.

Not everyone was preoccupied with doctrinal disputes. A deep Protestant spirituality found expression in some of the greatest hymn writing of the church's history and in devotional works in the tradition of Thomas à Kempis's *Imitation of Christ*. Some of the great classics of English literature were written during the period by the Puritans John Bunyan (1628–1688) and John Milton (1608–1674).

In Germany, where rigid state control of post-Reformation Lutheran churches stifled spirituality, a revival known as Pietism was born. Pietism was a highly personal approach to Christian faith that emphasized the Christian's post-conversion life as one of ongoing sanctification. Though it emphasized the individual believer's personal relationship with Christ, Pietism did not call for a total separation from the world. On the contrary, it called for Christians to become salt and light in the fallen world. The Pietists founded schools, orphanages, hospitals, libraries, and printing presses. One Pietist leader, August Hermann Francke (1663–1727), founded a press in 1710 that later became the Canstein Bible Society, the largest Bible distributor in eighteenth-century Europe. Both the Church of the Brethren and the Moravian Church sprang from German Pietism. The Moravian Church, led by Count Nicholas Ludwig von Zinzendorf (1700–1760), was destined to play a leading role in the birth of Protestant foreign missions during the eighteenth century.

THE CATHOLIC REFORMATION
. . . .

The Catholic Reformation was not simply a response to the Protestant Reformation. Like the Protestant Reformation, which it paralleled chronologically, it was partially rooted in fifteenth-century Christian humanism. Members of the Oratory of Divine Love, founded in Florence in 1497, embraced reform along the lines suggested by Erasmus and other Christian humanists. They believed that reform might come through the practice of love and moral improvement. What made the Oratory significant were the individuals who were attracted to it. By 1520, some sixty individuals, among them some of the most influential figures in the church, were members.

Among the noteworthy members of the Oratory were Reginald Pole, who served as Archbishop of Canterbury and advisor to Mary Tudor during her attempt to return England to the Catholic faith; Jacopo Sadoleto, who tried to lure Geneva back to Catholicism during Calvin's exile from Geneva (1538–1541); Gaetano da Thiene, who, together with Giovanni Pietro Caraffa, founded the Theatines, or Congregation of Clerics Regular in 1524, devoted to preaching, teaching, and social service; and most notably, Gasparo Contarini, who chaired the reform commission appointed by Pope Paul III (1534–1549) to recommend reforms and prepare the church for the Council of Trent.

Contarini and Caraffa were a study in contrasts that demonstrates the diversity within the Catholic Reformation. Gasparo Contarini, a well-educated scholar and diplomat, came from a wealthy Venetian family. In 1511, he experienced a religious conversion similar to Martin Luther's. In 1535, Pope Paul III made Contarini a cardinal and in 1536 asked him to chair the reform commission. The commission, which included Caraffa and Pole, presented its findings and recommendations to the pope in 1537 in the document known as the *Concilium,* or *Council on Reforming the Church.* The commission called for sweeping reforms from the papacy to the parish, but it did not, as the Protestant Reformers did, see any need for doctrinal reform.

Contarini was a peacemaker who shared some opinions with the Protestant Reformers and hoped to achieve a reconciliation with them. He apparently accepted salvation by grace alone as taught by Augustine. In 1541, Contarini served as papal legate at the Colloquy of Regensburg, where moderate Catholic theologians met with moderate Protestant theologians, most notably Philip Melanchthon. A young John Calvin was also present. The Colloquy was able to reach agreements on free will, original sin, and, most importantly, on justification by "faith and grace, dependent on the merits of Christ." The justifying faith was one made "lively and efficacious through works of charity."[19] The debate on the Lord's Supper deadlocked the Colloquy, however. Contarini refused to compromise on the doctrine of transubstantiation.

The agreements reached by Contarini and Melanchthon were repudiated by their colleagues back home. Contarini was accused of heresy upon his return to Rome. He died the following year. The Colloquy was also undermined by Francis I of France (1494–1547), who feared a religious settlement in Germany would enhance the power of the Hapsburgs. The conservatives were gaining the upper hand in Rome, displacing moderates like Contarini. Caraffa was one of the most important advocates of the new policy.

Giovanni Pietro Caraffa began his career as a chamberlain under Pope Alexander VI. By 1506, he was a bishop. While papal

---

[19] A. G. Dickens, *The Counter Reformation* (New York: Harcourt, Brace & World, 1969), 105.

envoy to Spain (1517–1520), he was much impressed by the workings of the Spanish Inquisition. Caraffa moved steadily away from his earlier, moderate positions until, by 1542, he was the most outspoken critic of those like Contarini, who sought reconciliation with the Protestants. Instead, Caraffa advocated combating Protestantism with every weapon available, especially the Inquisition. In anticipation of Pope Paul III's bull, *Licet ab Initio,* authorizing the reestablishment of the Inquisition in Italy, Caraffa used his own meager funds to rent and equip a dungeon in Rome. By application of terror and torture, all stirrings of Protestant or liberal Catholic thought in Italy were soon exterminated.

In 1555, Caraffa was elected Pope Paul IV (1555–1559), an event that made the courageous Ignatius Loyola "shake in every bone of his body."[20] Paul IV continued the Council of Trent called by Paul III. The council met in three main sessions between 1545 and 1563. Of the 270 bishops who attended this ecumenical council, 187 were Italians. Two were Germans. The remainder were from Spain and France. No attempt was made at reconciliation with the Protestants. In general, the Council of Trent reaffirmed Roman Catholic doctrine as it existed before the Protestant Reformation. Many of the more blatant abuses, such as the selling of indulgences, were dealt with. Bishops were instructed to reside in their dioceses and establish seminaries for the training of the clergy. A catechism was developed so that Catholics could distinguish truth from error. Thomas Aquinas was established as the dominant theological influence in the revitalized Catholic church. For the next four hundred years, until the Vatican II Council (1961–1965), the Catholic church would remain as defined at Trent.

In 1559, the year of his death, Paul IV issued the *Index of Prohibited Books.* An expanded *Index* was issued by the Council of Trent in 1564. About 75 percent of all books being published in Europe at the time were included. All of the works of Erasmus and all vernacular translations of the Bible were included. The *Index* was updated periodically until its abolition in 1966.

[20] Quoted in ibid., 90.

When Paul IV died, citizens in Rome sacked the headquarters of the Inquisition, burning its records. The College of Cardinals then elected Giovanni Angelo de Medici as Pius IV (1559–1565), who proved even more reactionary and ruthless than his predecessor. He soon smashed the Caraffa political faction in Rome and had its leaders executed.

If the papacy proved immune to real reform, those who desired to serve rather than be served found an outlet in the new monastic orders, like the Theatines, Barnabites, Capuchians, Carmelites, and most notably, the Society of Jesus, or Jesuits.

The founder of the Jesuits was Ignatius Loyola, a former Spanish soldier whose leg was shattered by a cannon ball in one of the many dynastic wars between Spain and France. While convalescing, Loyola spent his time reading books on the life of Christ and the lives of the saints. He was converted and vowed to become a soldier for Christ. He then spent a year in a monastery, during which he wrote *Spiritual Exercises,* a manual of instruction for four weeks of meditation and contemplation on sin and Jesus Christ's life, passion, and resurrection. Today, *Spiritual Exercises* remains a popular devotional guide for Catholics and Protestants alike. Loyola's year at Manresa Monastery has been compared with Luther's troubled search to find peace with God. Whereas Luther found his peace in the Bible, thus rejecting the teachings of the medieval church, Loyola embraced the medieval church.

Loyola soon had a following, but the road ahead was rocky. Twice he was imprisoned for suspected heresy. In 1537, he and five companions were ordained to the priesthood in Venice. Prevented from going on to Palestine when war broke out between the Republic of Venice and the Turks, they went instead to Rome, where Loyola again encountered charges of heresy. Unselfish service among the poor in Rome and the friendship of Gasparo Contarini won for Loyola and his followers recognition as the Society of Jesus by Pope Paul III in 1540.

The Jesuits concentrated on three tasks: education, winning back those areas lost to Protestantism, and foreign missions. In the field of education, they founded schools universally known for their excellence. The Jesuits became, and remain today, among the best educated Christian clergy. Organized along military lines and sworn to a special oath of absolute obedience to the pope, the Jesuits became the shock troops of the Catholic church's counteroffensive against Protestantism. They were largely responsible for halting the spread of Protestantism and winning back large areas previously lost to the Protestant Reformation. Their greatest and most heroic efforts were expended overseas evangelizing America, Africa, and Asia.

CATHOLIC MISSIONS TO THE WORLD[21]

. . . .

From the mid-fifteenth century through the sixteenth century, overseas exploration and discovery was dominated by the Iberian kingdoms of Spain and Portugal. From the beginning, the primary motivation was economic gain. But along with the desire for profits went a desire to Christianize the world. This dual motivation also ran true for the Dutch, English, and French, who began overseas exploration and colonization in earnest in the seventeenth century. Differences existed. For example, the Portuguese and Spanish ventures were sponsored by their governments, while those of their competitors were normally underwritten by government-chartered, private companies.

Since Spain and Portugal were both Catholic nations, wherever their explorers went, Jesuit missionaries usually went also. In 1493, Pope Alexander VI issued the papal bull *Inter cetera,* dividing the New World between Spain and Portugal and directing the Catholic monarchs to send to the New World "God-fearing, well-trained, and experienced men who would instruct the inhabitants there in the Catholic faith."[22]

As was mentioned earlier, profit was the primary motive behind the exploration and settlement of the New World. A sixteenth-century Spanish diplomat summed it up best when he

---

[21]For coverage of the early Catholic missions, I am indebted largely to the summary in Robert G. Clouse, et. al., *Two Kingdoms,* 293-316.
[22]Quoted in ibid., 299.

97

said, "Religion supplies the pretext and gold the motive."[23] In this conflict between serving God and seeking gold and glory, it fell upon the missionaries to restrain those for whom gold and glory were paramount—no easy task. The Spanish crown was given control of the churches in the New World. Missionaries and all other church personnel in the colonies were appointed by the state and could not communicate with the papacy except through the government.

The Jesuit Bartholomew de Las Casas was appointed protector general of the Indians by Cardinal Francisco Ximenez, the Grand Inquisitor of the Spanish Inquisition. Las Casas repeatedly pled the case of the Indians' humanity before the Spanish king, arguing against the settlers' assertions that they were subhuman and incapable of becoming Christians. The monarch was caught between viewing the Indians as his Christian subjects and viewing them as forced labor, essential for the economic survival of the colonies. As is so often the case in history, the economic arguments had more appeal than the humanitarian ones. It was a story repeated in the Portuguese colonies in Africa and Brazil, and later in the North American colonies, where Protestant missionaries tried to protect Christian Indians from land-hungry colonists.

Jesuits led the foreign mission effort in the Portuguese colonies, also. Of the many dedicated missionaries, the names of Francis Xavier and Matteo Ricci stand out. Francis Xavier answered the call of the Portuguese king for missionaries to go to Asia. Beginning in 1542, Xavier visited India, Ceylon, Malaya, the East Indies, and Japan. In 1552, after just ten years as a missionary, Xavier died of fever on an island off the coast of China. Perhaps his most successful efforts were expended in Japan, where he spent two years. By 1582, there existed a larger percentage of Japanese Christians than there are in Japan today.

In 1587, the Jesuits were joined by Franciscan missionaries from the Philippines. Unlike the Jesuits, who worked among the upper classes, the Franciscans worked among the poor. The gov-

---

[23]Quoted in John P. McKay, et. al., *A History of World Societies,* 3rd. ed. (Dallas: Houghton Mifflin Co., 1992), 570.

ernment became alarmed, fearing that the traditional social order was threatened. They also feared that the Spanish might have imperial ambitions in Japan. In 1614, the Shogun, Tokugawa Ieyasu, declared Christianity illegal, expelled the missionaries, martyred the Japanese Christians who would not give up their faith, and closed Japan to the outside world. Only the Dutch were allowed to send one ship per year to Japan for purposes of trade. Despite the severe persecution, the infant church survived underground, as families passed the gospel in secret from one generation to the next. When Japan was opened to the world in the 1850s, more than fifteen thousand Christians were found.

Xavier died while waiting to be allowed into China, but another Jesuit, Matteo Ricci, arrived in Peking (modern Beijing) in 1601. China had been exposed to Christianity during the seventh century by Nestorians and again around the beginning of the fourteenth century by Franciscans, but those groups were forced out in 1368. Ricci's success was due in part to his efforts to separate Christianity from European culture and his appeal to the upper classes, especially the Confucian scholars. He dressed like a Chinese scholar, studied the Confucian classics, learned the language, and wrote about Christianity and Western science in Chinese.

The papacy both aided and hindered the missionaries. Pope Gregory XV (1621–1623) set up the Congregation for the Propagation of the Faith ("Propaganda" for short) in 1622. The Propaganda studied the best methods for propagating the faith in foreign lands, selected and trained missionaries, and did many of the detailed tasks undertaken by modern missionary societies. One emphasis was the development of indigenous clergy. In 1626, the Propaganda established a printing press. By the end of the eighteenth century it was publishing books in more than forty foreign languages. The Jesuit Alexander de Rhodes created a written language for the people of Indochina (Vietnam). Contacts that de Rhodes made with a group of priests in Paris led to the founding of the Foreign Missionary Society in 1663. It took as its mission the promotion of indigenous churches in Southeastern Asia—native clergy serving under native bishops. Such enlightened efforts were limited, however, since the papacy was never able to get control of missions in the Spanish and Portuguese empires.

In one sense, the papacy undermined the success of missions in Asia when it took sides in the "Rites Controversy" in India and China. The missionaries tried to distinguish between the message and its cultural trappings, both with respect to Christianity and the native religions. In China, for example, the Jesuits allowed their converts to continue venerating the memory of Confucius and their ancestors as nonreligious social and political practices. When the Dominicans and Franciscans began working in China, they opposed the Jesuits, accusing them of compromising with pagan religious practices. When the controversy was referred to the papacy, the pope sided against the Jesuits. In the meantime, the debate between the missionaries discredited Christianity in the eyes of many Chinese. That, together with fear of Western imperialism, led to the proscription of Christianity in China in 1724. Persecution followed, but nothing as severe as in Japan. By 1800, the number of Chinese Christians was reduced to about half of what it was at the beginning of the century.

The history of Catholic missions during the sixteenth and seventeenth centuries is one of the heroic and inspiring chapters in church history. By the end of the eighteenth century, however, Catholic missions were largely at a standstill. This was due in part to the decline of the Spanish and Portuguese empires, to which these early mission efforts were tied. Another cause was the eventual dissolution of the Society of Jesus in 1773—a victim of the Enlightenment. With the disappearance of the Jesuits, the church lost its most enthusiastic and effective missionary force. Tragically, the native Christians in Latin America lost their protection and were left at the mercy of those European settlers who saw their exploitation as a means to greater profits. Yet all was not lost, for by the dawn of the nineteenth century, Protestants were beginning to catch the vision for foreign missions.

RELIGIOUS WARS

. . . .

The Reformation and the division of Europe into Catholics and Protestants provided the backdrop for a series of wars, often referred to as the "wars of religion." The rise of Spanish power due to its New World empire and strong, national religious unity fueled the flames. In these religious wars, religious loyalties were readily abandoned when in conflict with dynastic interests. For example, Catholic France allied with the infidel Turks against the Catholic Hapsburgs (Holy Roman Empire), gave aid to the Protestant princes against the Catholic princes within the Holy Roman Empire in the Schmalkaldic War (1546–1555), and joined forces with the Protestants in the Thirty Years' War (1617–1648), insuring the defeat of the Catholic Hapsburgs and preventing the unification of Germany under Hapsburg rule.

The mix of religious and dynastic motives was more obvious in the religious wars in France between 1562 and 1598. This is evident in an observation made by the ambassador to France from the Republic of Venice at the time: "Into the whole body [of France] there has been introduced the curse of the new sects which has totally confused the religion of the realm, which is the sole means of holding a people united and obedient to its prince."[24] This widely held belief was a root cause of the religious intolerance of the time—especially toward the Anabaptists. In France, Protestants (known as Huguenots) represented a threat to the kingdom, because the religious conflict became wrapped up in the struggle over the throne.

With the death of Henry II in 1559, his widow, Catherine de Medici, served as regent for their three sons, who ruled in succession as Francis II (d.1560), Charles IX (d. 1574), and Henry III (d. 1589). It was obvious to all that none of these royal oddities would produce an heir, and the Valois dynasty would die with them. The next heir to the throne was Henry Bourbon, Duke of Navarre. But Henry was a Huguenot, and a Protestant king

[24]Quoted in James B. Ross and Mary M. McLoughlin, eds., *The Portable Renaissance Reader* (New York: Viking, 1953), 319.

was unacceptable to the Catholic majority. Catholics rallied around Henry, Duke of Guise, who also had a claim to the throne. A series of civil wars was fought over whether a Protestant Bourbon or a Catholic Guise dynasty would succeed the Valois.

The conflict reached a climax during the War of the Three Henrys (1588–1589). Henry III arranged the assassination of Henry of Guise in December 1588. Six months later, he was himself assassinated by a fanatical monk, but not before naming Henry of Navarre as his heir. So, Henry of Navarre, a Huguenot, became Henry IV. The Catholics, unwilling to accept a "heretic" as their king, enlisted aid from Philip II (1527–1598) of Spain, who hoped to put a Spanish Catholic on the French throne. The Catholics continued the war and prevented Henry IV from occupying his capital, Paris. Finally, in 1593, Henry converted to Catholicism commenting that "Paris is worth a Mass." The French wars of religion ended. Bourbons would occupy the French throne until the end of the monarchy in 1830.

Once in power in Paris, Henry IV issued the Edict of Nantes (1598), granting limited religious tolerance to the Huguenots. To some, the terms of the edict created the impossible situation of a state within a state. As absolutism developed under Henry's successors, Louis XIII (1601–1643) and Louis XIV (1638–1715), the terms of the Edict of Nantes were steadily broken until 1685, when Louis XIV revoked it. Huguenots were given the choice of fleeing France, converting to Catholicism, or serving as galley slaves in the French Mediterranean fleet.

In the civil war that broke out in Germany in 1617, there was a curious mix of religious and dynastic motives as well. Protestants in Bohemia attempted to prevent the Catholic Hapsburg Emperor Ferdinand II (1578–1637) from becoming King of Bohemia—his right by inheritance. The Protestant forces were soundly defeated at the Battle of White Mountain near Prague in 1620. This Catholic victory upset the balance of power in Europe. Christian IV, the Protestant king of Denmark, entered the conflict in 1625 to protect the Protestant princes of northern

Germany from being engulfed by the victorious Catholic Hapsburgs. He, too, was defeated in 1629.

In 1630, the Lutheran king of Sweden, Gustavus Adolphus, wanting to make the Baltic Sea his own, establishing Sweden as a great power in Europe, took up the Protestant cause. A brilliant general, he was unfortunately killed at the Battle of Lutzen (1632). Protestant fortunes began to wane once again. Cardinal Richelieu, leader of France as Louis XIII's chief minister, feared for the future of France, since it was surrounded by Hapsburgs in Spain and in Germany. France entered the war on the side of the Protestant princes. Previously, Catholic France had provided financial aid to the Protestants. Protestant Dutch bankers were not above providing financial support for both Protestant and Catholic armies. Such was the confusion of religious and political motives.

French involvement shifted the balance in favor of the Protestants. The war ended in 1648 with the Peace of Westphalia. Calvinism and Lutheranism were recognized in the Empire, and the independence of the Swiss Confederation and the United Provinces (Protestant Holland) was recognized. Recognition of the sovereignty of each individual political entity within the Holy Roman Empire prevented the unification of Germany until 1871.

The English Civil War (1640–1660; 1688–1689) was a religious war with a different twist. When Elizabeth I died in 1603, she was succeeded by James I (1566–1625), the first of the Stuart dynasty. James wanted to establish absolutism in England. He ran into opposition from a powerful, largely Puritan group within Parliament who wanted to establish a constitutional monarchy in England. Both forms of government were revolutionary ideas, for England was neither before 1603. Religion became a major issue in the ensuing conflict between the early Stuarts (James I and Charles I) and the Parliamentarians. The Stuarts felt that only an episcopal form of church government was compatible with an absolute monarchy, so they attempted to force religious conformity within the Church of England. The Parliamentarians saw constitutional government as a logical extension of the congregational or presbyterian governments found in their churches.

War broke out in 1640 when Charles I (1600–1649) tried to force Anglicanism onto Presbyterian Scotland. By 1642, the war with Scotland had become a civil war between the Parliamentarians (Roundheads) and supporters of the king (Cavaliers). Oliver Cromwell (1599–1658), a Puritan member of the gentry, took command of the New Model Army and in 1645, at the Battle of Naseby, the Cavaliers were decisively defeated. While negotiations with Charles I were under way, conflict broke out between the conservatives. Some wanted a constitutional monarchy but no further changes, while others wanted a more thorough transformation of English society. These "radicals" (called Independents, Levellers, and Diggers), together with the rank and file of the New Model Army, called for religious tolerance and a democratic political system allowing for universal male suffrage.

In 1648, Cromwell, himself a conserative, led a military coup against Parliament. He purged Parliament of all but fifty to sixty loyal followers. It was this "Rump" Parliament that tried Charles I for treason. The execution of Charles I on January 30, 1649, was unpopular with most Englishmen—even the Parliamentarians. Finding it no easier to govern with his Rump Parliament than Charles I had with his, Cromwell took the title "Lord Protector" and ruled England as a military dictator, despite a constitution that defined England as a commonwealth. When Cromwell died in 1658, leading Parliamentarians opened negotiations with Charles II (1630–1685) for a restoration of the monarchy. On May 29, 1660, Charles II returned from exile in France. He was welcomed home by cheering crowds and his path to the royal palace at Whitehall was strewn with flowers.

More than monarchy was restored to England in 1660. The "Cavalier Parliament," elected in 1661, passed legislation that severely restricted the liberties of Catholics, Puritans, and other so-called "Nonconformists," who would not take Communion according to the Anglican rite. In 1673, the Test Act was passed, which barred all Catholics and Dissenters from any civil or military office. It was aimed in part at Charles II's brother, James, the Duke of York, who openly professed Catholicism. Having spent their exile in France at the court of Louis XIV, Charles and James returned to England sympathetic to both Catholicism and absolutism.

During his reign, Charles II avoided an open break with Parliament. Only on his deathbed did he confess Catholicism. James II (1633–1701) ascended the throne in 1685. He soon began to promote Catholics within the government and the military. Many hoped that the aging monarch's reign would be brief and followed by a Protestant succession. But when a son was born to James II and his Catholic wife in June 1688, England was faced with a certain Catholic succession. Whig (Puritan) and Tory (Anglican) factions in Parliament joined forces and invited James II's Protestant daughter by a previous marriage, Mary, and her husband, William of Orange, grandson of Charles I, to invade and rescue England from Catholicism. James II, finding himself without support, fled to France. Parliament declared the throne vacant, and offered it to William and Mary as joint constitutional monarchs. Of course, they accepted.

This "Glorious" or "Bloodless Revolution" was concluded by a series of Parliamentary acts that established constitutional rule and religious liberty for all but Catholics, Unitarians, and Jews. In 1701, Parliament passed legislation that barred any Catholic from succession to the throne—aimed at the heirs of James II. The whole affair found theoretical justification in John Locke's social contract theory of government expounded in *Two Treatises of Government* (1690). Locke's theory later became the single most important influence in the drafting of the American Constitution.

TIMELINE FOR CHAPTER 6

1540	Society of Jesus (Jesuits) recognized
1542–1552	Francis Xavier, missionary to Asia
1545–1563	Council of Trent
1562–1589	Religious wars in France
1589	Edict of Nantes

1601	Matteo Ricci arrives in Peking (Beijing)
1614	Christianity is declared illegal in Japan
1618–1648	Thirty Years' War
1640–1645	Puritan Revolution in England
1648	Peace of Westphalia
1688	Glorious Revolution in England

CHAPTER SEVEN
The Challenge of Reason and Enlightenment: The Church during the Eighteenth Century

THE BIG PICTURE

The eighteenth century was a momentous era for both the church and secular society. The Scientific Revolution, launched by Nicolaus Copernicus in 1543 and culminating with the publication of Sir Isaac Newton's *Principia* in 1687, viewed the universe as a machine. The intellectuals of the eighteenth-century Enlightenment accepted this mechanistic view of the universe. They banished God from his creation by relegating him to the role of a clock maker, setting in motion, but remaining uninvolved with his creation. Autonomous reason and unbridled skepticism characterized intellectual life during the century. The growth of a mechanistic view of the universe developed alongside the growth of Protestant orthodoxy, which also emphasized reason and downplayed emotions. The result was spiritual famine in the churches. But the Lord had not abandoned his church, and at the beginning of the century, he sent revival throughout the churches. Individuals, often the least likely candidates for greatness, like Nicholaus von Zinzendorf, Jonathan Edwards, George Whitefield, and John Wesley were the willing instruments of revival in Europe and North America. Not only were the churches called back to the preaching of the gospel, but through the work of Zinzendorf and the Moravian Brethren, the modern foreign missions movement was founded.

KEY EVENTS

1687	The publication of Sir Isaac Newton's *Principia* provides a mechanistic model of the universe that remains valid until the twentieth century.
1730s	Revival breaks out in America and Britain through the preaching of John Wesley, George Whitefield, and Jonathan Edwards.
1732	The first Moravian missionaries are sent out from Herrnhut, thus beginning the modern (Protestant) foreign missions movement.
1751	The new secular worldview of modernity triumphs in part through the publication of the *Encyclopedia*.
1789	The outbreak of the French Revolution signals the end of the "Old Order" and the birth of the modern political and social order.

On May 24, 1543, the Polish astronomer Nicolaus Copernicus died at Frauenburg, the northernmost Catholic diocese in Poland. As he lay dying, he was handed a copy of his book, *On the Revolutions of the Celestial Spheres,* which had just been printed. The publication of Copernicus's book was not the only great publishing event of that year. In England, *A Necessary Doctrine and Erudition for a Christian Man,* commonly called *King Henry's Book,* was also published. In Geneva, John Calvin published a revised Latin edition of the *Institutes of the Christian Religion,* and in Paris, Peter Ramus published his reformed version of Aristotle's logic, *Animadversiones Aristotelicae,* which was promptly condemned by the faculty of the Sorbonne at the University of Paris. But it was the publication of Copernicus's book that is commonly taken as marking the transition from the medieval (premodern) to the scientific (modern) view of the universe. Christian scholars view it as the beginning of the abandonment of a Christian (or biblical) worldview, completed during the eighteenth-century "Enlightenment."

According to the medieval view of the universe, the earth sat immobile at the center of the universe. Above and around the earth was a series of crystalline spheres in which were embedded the moon, planets, and stars. The planets themselves were perfect spheres composed of a divine ether. The outermost sphere was the "prime mover" that drove all the others. The spheres revolved around the earth every twenty-four hours. Beyond the prime mover was the heavenly abode, where God, the angels, and the heavenly host resided.

All of God's creation was in an ascending order, or hierarchy. Somewhere within the earth was hell, as far removed from God as possible. The earth itself was the abode of fallen mankind, created in God's image but separated from him by sin. Then there was the ascending order of planets, until one reached the heavenly abode. Similarly, one could see a hierarchical order as one moved from rocks (existence), to plants (existence plus life), to animals (existence, life, and motion), to mankind (created in God's image with the ability to reason), to the angels and heavenly host. There was even a hierarchy in society. God created peasants to work the fields, nobles to govern and hunt, and clergy to pray. On the earth, everything consisted of the four basic elements—earth, water, air, fire—also in an ascending order. In order for there to be life, all four elements had to be present. For that life to be healthy, they had to be balanced.

The medieval world was psychologically a very comfortable world in which to live. Everything made sense. Each individual knew exactly where he or she fit in God's great chain of being. The individual knew why he or she was created, that is, the purpose and meaning of one's life. Never before, and certainly never since Copernicus, has everything made so much sense.

This very comfortable, pleasant worldview was the product of the medieval synthesis—that reconciliation of the Bible and classical philosophy (especially Aristotle) achieved during the High Middle Ages by Thomas Aquinas and the other scholastic theologians. It rested upon the acceptance of authority. It answered the question of *why* things were as they were. No one was really asking the question of *how* things worked. No one was seeking truth as if it was something to be discovered. The truth was already known. It could be found in the writings of

Plato, Aristotle, Claudius Ptolemy, Galen, and the other known great works of antiquity. The church accepted this wealth of knowledge as being in harmony with the Bible, and it was not to be questioned. Aristotle, for example, taught that the earth was motionless in the center of the universe. This could be verified by observation, made perfect sense logically, and was emotionally very pleasing.

Given the fact that the earth was at the center of the universe, the scholar's task was to demonstrate this truth, or what followed from it, by a process of deductive reasoning. What one did not do—and dared not do—was ask the question of whether or not the earth was in fact at the center of the universe and then try to discover the answer to that question. That was what Copernicus did, and by so doing he destroyed the medieval synthesis and the comfort and certainty that it provided. It was one of the greatest intellectual revolutions in history.

Copernicus was not trying to destroy the medieval synthesis. In fact, he was trying to preserve it—at least its earth-centered (geocentric) model of the universe. But Copernicus was working under the assumption that the simpler something was, the more likely it was to be true, and the geocentric model of the universe was very difficult to explain mathematically. Copernicus discovered that the order of the planets made much more sense mathematically by simply placing the sun at the center with the earth revolving around it, and the moon revolving around the earth. That is the only change he made. He kept the crystalline spheres and the twenty-four hour revolution of the planets. But that one little correction was enough to destroy the whole medieval view of reality and of what was true or false.

To understand how serious the implications of Copernicus's minor correction were to the medieval mind, the Christian should consider what the implications would be if the Bible was proved to be not the infallible word of God, but only a faulty collection of ancient legends and myths. What would it mean for our understanding as Christians of who we are, who God is, and what the meaning and purpose of life is—if any? Similarly, for the individuals of Copernicus's day to question the truth of the order of the universe was to question all truth. If the church was wrong about the planets, what else did it have wrong? When Martin Luther was informed of Copernicus's theory, he commented: "This fool wishes to reverse the entire science of astronomy; but the sacred Scripture tells us that Joshua commanded the sun to stand still and not the earth."[25]

After Copernicus, Johannes Kepler (1571–1630), a German astronomer, discovered the laws of planetary motion. He was able to demonstrate mathematically that the orbits of the planets were elliptical, not circular, and that their speed varied with their distance from the sun. Kepler's significance lay in his use of mathematical proofs. A mechanistic view of the universe was beginning to emerge.

The Italian mathematician, Galileo Galilei (1564–1642), went a giant step further. Galileo believed that the whole of nature was governed by certain universal truths, or natural laws, that could be verified mathematically. Whereas Aristotle and the medieval scholastic philosophers relied on *a priori* principles and common sense, Galileo advocated direct observation and mathematics as the means to achieving knowledge about nature. Galileo argued that nature in its most minute details, whether an atom or a planet, displayed mathematical regularity. For Galileo, the universe was rational, but it was the rationality of mathematics, not scholastic logic. What was real was what could be measured.

The discoveries and theories of Copernicus, Kepler, and Galileo were brought together in the theory of universal gravity, discovered by Sir Isaac Newton (1642–1727), an eccentric genius and professor of mathematics at Cambridge University in England. Newton published his theory in *The Mathematical Principles of Natural Philosophy* (1687), or *Principia* for short, one of the most influential books ever published. According to Newton, the universe is like a machine, with all of its parts working together harmoniously. For Newton and the other scientists of his day, this mechanistic view of the universe did not present a

---

[25] Quoted in *Two Kingdoms*, 368.

problem for religion. God was a rational God. Humans created in God's image were rational beings who could discover and understand how God's universe worked. For Newton, the universe was a uniformity of cause-and-effect natural law, but it was an open system—God could and did intervene in his creation. When Newton considered the universe, he was struck by the majesty of God displayed in it. He wrote:

> This most beautiful system of the sun, planets, and comets could only proceed from the counsel and dominion of an intelligent and powerful Being. And if the fixed stars are the centers of other like systems, these being formed by the like wise counsel, must be all subject to the dominion of the One. . . . This Being governs all things . . . as Lord over all. . . . The Supreme God is a Being eternal, infinite, absolutely perfect. . . . He endures forever and is everywhere present.[26]

The intellectuals who came after the early scientists during this period known as the Enlightenment, or Age of Reason (the late-seventeenth and eighteenth centuries), were impressed with the mechanistic view of the universe—so much so that they questioned the necessity of God's involvement in his creation. They did not question the existence of God, for if the universe is like a clock, then it is only reasonable to assume that there is a clock maker. Not only that, but any denial of the existence of a creator would raise the question of whether there is any meaning for history, for the individual, for anything. For God to intervene in his creation, however, would violate natural law, they believed. Therefore, they opted for a view of the universe as a uniformity of cause-and-effect natural law within a closed system. Their religion was Deism.

The god of the Deists was not the personal, infinite, triune God

---

[26]Quoted in Marvin Perry, *An Intellectual History of Modern Europe* (Dallas: Houghton Mifflin Company, 1992), 81.

of the Bible, acting in history. Their god was the great architect, or clock maker, who created the universe and then withdrew from it, leaving humans to act within it, guided only by the light of reason. They believed that what can be known of "nature's God" was found in the study of his creation. Since miracles were believed to violate natural law, they were dismissed as superstition. Only that which could be proven by the application of reason (the scientific method) was true. That which could not be so proven was either false or irrelevant. What Christians saw as the effects of sin in a fallen world, the Enlightenment understood to be the corruption of naturally good people by history, poor education, and faulty institutions. Since humans were by nature good and able to reason, it followed that by discovering the natural laws of society, people could correct the faulty institutions and create a utopia on earth. Thus the intellectuals of the Enlightenment believed in progress. They were optimistic about the future because of their faith in the perfectibility of humanity.

Skepticism was another characteristic of the Enlightenment and was fostered by both the Scientific Revolution and the Protestant Reformation. The Scientific Revolution challenged the church by substituting a clockwork universe for the divinely ordered universe portrayed in Dante's *Divine Comedy*. The Protestant Reformation also challenged the authority of the church in the name of a higher authority, the Bible, but left many wondering if religious truth could be known for certain. Who interprets the Bible? The century of Protestant scholasticism did not seem to help. Rather, it emphasized the potential differences of interpretation.

Skepticism was also encouraged by the increased contact with non-Western civilizations. Exploration and worldwide seaborne commerce brought Europeans into intimate contact with Asian civilizations that were more ancient than theirs. India, China, and Japan, for example, had civilizations with urban centers, social and economic classes, and highly developed religious philosophies while Europeans were still living in primitive tribal societies. This exposure to non-Christian religions led to the conviction that all religious beliefs, whether Christian, Hindu, or

Buddhist, were only superstition—equally true and equally false. This religious skepticism led to tolerance, and contributed to the rise of religious liberty. Gone was the passionate concern for truth that had earlier led to the persecution of those labeled as heretics.

The Enlightenment was an international movement centered in Paris, France. Its followers in France were known collectively as *philosophes.* They included such figures as Voltaire (1694–1778), Montesquieu (1689–1755), Denis Diderot (1713–1784), Jean d'Alembert (1717–1783), and Jean-Jacques Rousseau (1712–1778). Outside France, John Locke (1632–1704), Adam Smith (1732–1790), David Hume (1711–1776), Gottfried Wilhelm Leibnitz (1646–1716), Immanuel Kant (1724–1804), Benjamin Franklin (1706–1790), and Thomas Jefferson (1743–1826) stand out as leading advocates of the new worldview. That Franklin and Jefferson were equally at home among the *literati* of Europe as they were among the colonists in Philadelphia or Virginia is a measure of the cosmopolitan nature of the Enlightenment. Most of the founding fathers of the American republic were adherents of the Enlightenment and the Deistic view of the universe, including George Washington (1732–1799) and Thomas Paine (1737–1809).

The Enlightenment intellectuals were propagandists. They wanted to communicate their new secular worldview to the literate public. Education, they believed, was the key to fine-tuning the universe machine on the way to utopia. Many of them contributed to the multivolume *Encyclopedia,* edited by Denis Diderot and Jean d'Alembert. Few publications in modern history have been so influential. The editors stated from the beginning that their purpose was to "change the way people think." Although it was condemned by the churches and censored in France, the *Encyclopedia* was found in the libraries of the literate in both Europe and America, including Catholic and Protestant clergy.

It is against the background of the Enlightenment and the century of Protestant scholasticism and orthodoxy that one must understand the revivals that swept across Europe and North

America in the late-seventeenth and eighteenth centuries. In one sense they were, like romanticism, a reaction to the overemphasis on reason among the intellectuals of the Enlightenment. People are more than machines. Each individual has a personality that longs for personal relationships, ultimately with the One in whose image each individual is created. There is an emotional side to people that cannot be explained or satisfied by the scientific method.

Deism also failed to satisfy the inner longing of people for meaning. One cannot have a personal relationship with a clock maker God, who exists silent somewhere outside the universe, anymore than modern human beings can have a personal relationship with a computer. The Enlightenment based its optimism on the illusion that humans are by nature good; but history and experience demonstrate otherwise. If the universe is as it was created, then there is no reason to believe that either God or humanity is good by nature. Thus the leading intellectuals of the Enlightenment displayed a contempt for the very creatures, human beings, whom their worldview sought to ennoble. Voltaire spoke of "men as a lot of insects, devouring one another on a drop of mud."[27] The universe only makes sense in light of God's revelation—that it is a fallen world. And not only this explanation, but also the remedy, are to be found in God's revelation.

The cold orthodoxy of the seventeenth-century Protestant churches deadened the soul and stifled the spirit. Too often infant baptism, described by some as a "mark of the covenant," or "baptism into the covenant community," was misunderstood as a guarantee of conversion. Giving intellectual assent to a memorized catechism took the place of a real conversion experience. Conversion is more than an intellectual assent to right doctrine. It is a personal relationship with the risen Lord Jesus Christ. It involves emotions. Correct doctrine without a personal relationship with Jesus Christ is like faith without works—dead!

[27] Roland H. Bainton, *Christendom: A Short History of Christianity and Its Impact on Western Civilization, vol. 2, from the Reformation to the Present* (New York: Harper & Row, 1964), 110.

REVIVALS
. . . .

The great revival of the early-eighteenth century was wide-spread. In Germany and Scandinavia, where it began in the Lutheran state churches, it was known as Pietism. The Pietists stressed a new birth and personal relationship with Jesus Christ, a lifestyle of moral purity, a daily routine of prayer and Bible study, service to the less fortunate, and evangelism at home and abroad. Its origins are usually associated with the work of Philip Spener and August Hermann Franke. Perhaps the best known of the Pietist leaders was Count Nicholaus Ludwig von Zinzendorf, founder of the Moravian Brethren.

In England, the revival was called Evangelicalism and in North America, the Great Awakening. Among Roman Catholics in Europe, it was called Quietism. In England and America, it was a revival within the spiritless bodies of the Anglican and Reformed (Calvinist) churches. The leading figures were Jonathan Edwards (1703–1758), George Whitefield (1714–1770), and John Wesley (1703–1791). Whitefield's preaching on both sides of the Atlantic linked the two revivals. Zinzendorf was the link between German Pietism and the English-speaking revivals, as well as the link between the revivals and the first great Protestant foreign mission movement.

ZINZENDORF AND THE MORAVIANS
. . . .

Nicholaus Ludwig von Zinzendorf's father died from tuberculosis when Ludwig was only six weeks old. When his mother remarried three years later, Ludwig was sent to live with his maternal grandmother. The three women who profoundly influenced his life—his mother, his grandmother, and his mother's sister—were all devout Christians and Pietists.

In December 1722 a group of ten Bohemian Brethren, six adults and four children, arrived at Berthelsdorf, Zinzendorf's estate. They were a remnant of the United Brethren Church (*Unitas Fratrum*), founded in 1457 by followers of Jan Hus.

Zinzendorf allowed the refugees to settle on his estate. Soon other religious refugees arrived, including former Catholics, Anabaptists, Separatists, Schwenkfelders, Reformed, and even Lutherans. By 1726, the community of Herrnhut ("The Lord's Watch") numbered three hundred souls. In 1727, Zinzendorf resigned from his position at the Danish court and devoted the rest of his life to nurturing the Christian community at Herrnhut and the missionary movement that began there.

Zinzendorf never meant for the community at Herrnhut to develop into a denomination. The Brethren at Herrnhut took Communion regularly from the local Lutheran minister prior to 1734, the year Zinzendorf was ordained as a Lutheran minister. Zinzendorf was thoroughly ecumenical in his approach to Christianity. He believed that all churches were a part of the one true church, the body of Christ. Rejecting both the rationalism of the secular world and the dead orthodox scholasticism of the churches, he believed that Christians could experience unity across denominational lines through what he called "heart religion," a stress upon the emotional and experiential side of religion. Many scholars regard Zinzendorf as the father of the modern ecumenical movement.

The deep devotion to following Christ that characterized Pietism in general, and the Christians at Herrnhut in particular, is evident in many of the two thousand hymns written by Zinzendorf (e.g., "Jesus Still Lead On, Till Our Rest Be Won,") and in his declaration to the Herrnhut community: "I have only one passion. It is He, none but He."[28] It is also evident in an around-the-clock prayer meeting that began on August 27, 1727, and continued unbroken for over one hundred years. The year 1727 has come to be regarded as the birth year of the Renewed Moravian Church. It was recognized as a denomination separate from the Lutheran church in 1742.

Zinzendorf felt an obligation to take the gospel to the unbelieving multitude in the farthest reaches of the globe. While

---

[28]Quoted in Bruce L. Shelley, *Church History in Plain Language* (Waco, TX: Word, Inc., 1982), 348.

attending the coronation of Christian VI (1699–1746) as King of Denmark in 1731, Zinzendorf met a former slave from the Danish West India Islands. Out of that meeting came the desire to carry the gospel to the African slaves in the New World. When he presented the vision to the community at Herrnhut, there was an enthusiastic response. On August 21, 1732, the first Moravian missionaries, Leonhard Dober and David Nitschmann, set sail for St. Thomas Island. Others followed. By 1750, there were 175 missionaries serving in various parts of Africa, Asia, North America, and even Lapland and Greenland. By 1832, there were forty-two Moravian mission stations around the world. They were pioneers in missions to the Jews. During the heyday of Moravian missions, they could boast of having one missionary in the field for every sixty church members.

Between 1736 and 1747, Zinzendorf was banished from Saxony for his sectarian activities. During his banishment he traveled widely, founding Moravian communities in Europe, England, and America. While in the American colonies, he helped found Bethlehem, Pennsylvania, and personally preached to the Native Americans. The example set by Zinzendorf and the Moravians encouraged the Baptists to begin a foreign mission work in 1792. The annual Herrnhut Ministers Conference, inspired by Zinzendorf, led directly to the founding of the London Missionary Society in 1795 and the British and Foreign Bible Society in 1804. Perhaps the most far-reaching influence of Zinzendorf and the Moravians was achieved through the conversion of John Wesley.

The Methodist Revival

If Pietism was the means by which God brought revival to Lutheranism, then Methodism was the means he chose to bring revival to the Anglican and Nonconformist churches of England. The Puritan zeal that had led to the Puritan Revolution in the 1640s was hardly a memory by the early-eighteenth century. Sermons of the day were little more than moral platitudes that were more boring than inspiring. The doctrines of humanity's sinfulness, the Fall, and atonement were largely ignored. Church leaders like the Archbishop of Canterbury, John Tillotson, denounced "enthusiasm." The message was not the need for conversion but the need to "be generous, humane and tolerant, and avoid bigotry and fanaticism."[29] Truly, there was a famine in the land—a famine for the gospel, boldly preached.

John Wesley was born in 1703, the fifteenth of nineteen children born to Reverend Samuel Wesley, a High Church Anglican, and his wife, Susanna, the daughter of a Nonconformist minister. Susanna was a remarkable woman. She found time to give each of her children, whom she homeschooled, individual religious instruction every week. Her methodical nature left a lasting impression on John, who looked to her for guidance as long as she lived.

In 1720, John Wesley entered Oxford University and was elected a fellow of Lincoln College in 1726. Two years later, he was ordained an Anglican minister and spent two years assisting his father in the Epworth parish. When he returned to his duties at Oxford University, he joined a group of students organized by his brother Charles (1707–1788) to combat the spread of Deism at the university. The members of the group, among whom was George Whitefield, were called in derision "Methodists" by others at the university. They stressed a lifestyle of self-discipline that emphasized regular prayer, Bible study, and attendance at Communion.

From 1735 to 1737, Wesley served as a chaplain in the colony of Georgia. It was by all accounts a disastrous experience. However, on the voyage to Georgia, Wesley made the acquaintance of some Moravians, who were also going to America. Wesley was impressed by their humble spirit and cheerful manner. During a storm at sea when Wesley feared that he might die, he noticed that none of the Moravians—adults or children—were afraid. In fact, they sang during the storm. They did not fear death as Wesley did. Through the ministry of a young Moravian

[29]Ibid., 352.

minister by the name of Peter Bohler, Wesley learned that what he needed was a personal experience of God's forgiveness, the true meaning of the doctrine of justification by faith.

Back in London on May 24, 1738, Wesley accepted an invitation to attend a meeting at a Moravian chapel in Altersgate Street. There, as he later wrote, at a quarter before nine he experienced the new birth in Jesus Christ: "I felt my heart strangely warmed. I felt that I did trust in Christ, Christ alone, for salvation; and an assurance was given me that he had taken away *my* sins, even *mine,* and saved me from the law of sin and death."[30] Two days earlier, Charles Wesley had also experienced the new birth.

Like Luther and so many others before and since, John Wesley could not remain silent. He felt compelled to preach what he called "the glad tidings of salvation" to anyone who would listen. He visited Herrnhut and read Jonathan Edwards' account of the outbreak of revival in New England. Then, in the spring of 1739, Wesley accepted an invitation from George Whitefield to join him in open-air preaching to the coal miners in Bristol.

The suffering working classes of England had been largely ignored by the Anglican church. Whitefield, who by all accounts was one of the truly great orators of the period, found among the miners a hunger for the gospel. Wesley accepted Whitefield's invitation in part because he was finding the churches closed to his new enthusiastic preaching. Later, when he sought to preach in his father's old parish church at Epworth, he was barred from the pulpit and had to preach standing on his father's tomb in the church's graveyard.

Bristol was a turning point for Wesley. After Bristol, Wesley made the world his parish. He went wherever people would listen. From a study of his journals, historians calculate that he must have traveled two hundred fifty thousand miles, mostly on horseback, and preached an estimated forty-two thousand sermons. His brother, Charles, wrote over seven thousand hymns that were sung at Methodist meetings. Some of his hymns,

[30]Quoted in ibid., 355.

"Jesus, Lover of My Soul" and "Hark! The Herald Angels Sing," remain enduring favorites.

Like Zinzendorf, who resisted founding a new denomination, John Wesley remained a lifelong Anglican. In 1744, the first Annual Conference of Methodist preachers was held in London. In 1772, Wesley sent Francis Asbury to America—a stroke of genius. When Asbury arrived, there were only three Methodist meeting houses and three hundred members. Asbury organized the preachers as circuit riders and himself traveled an average of five thousand miles per year on horseback. During the American Revolution, when all other Methodist preachers returned to England (John Wesley was a Tory and a loyalist), Asbury remained and supported the Revolution. By the time of his death in 1816, there were 214,235 Methodists in 412 societies. In 1784, they organized as the Methodist Episcopal Church. The English Methodists did not formally organize as a church until 1795, four years after John Wesley's death.

THE GREAT AWAKENING IN AMERICA

. . . .

By the first quarter of the eighteenth century, the spiritual vision of many Americans had waned. Earthly prosperity became the main interest. It was to be expected in Virginia—from the beginning a boom colony growing rich from tobacco. But it was also true in New England among the Puritans, despite the preaching of Cotton Mather (1663–1728), the last great Puritan theologian, who, like Jeremiah of the Old Testament, continually called the people back to God. New Englanders grew prosperous from commerce, including the infamous slave trade. One measure of the spiritual famine among the descendants of the Puritans was the emergence of the Halfway Covenant.

The Halfway Covenant was an attempt to accommodate the many New England Congregationalists who could not give testimony of conversion, despite having been baptized as infants. Since voting rights were linked to church membership, in 1662, the Massachusetts Synod ruled that adults who lived an "upright life" could be admitted as members. Their children were baptized as "halfway" members, but were barred from taking Communion. Soon, that too changed, as ministers like Jonathan Edwards' grandfather, Solomon Stoddard, began admitting the unconverted to Communion. The spiritual life of the churches and the colonies suffered as the churches were filled with baptized, morally upright, but unconverted, "halfway Christians."

The Great Awakening is usually traced back to Theodore Frelinghuysen, a pastor in the Dutch Reformed Church in the Raritan Valley of New Jersey, who preached the need for a spiritual revival during the 1720s. The revival broke out with the preaching of Gilbert Tennent, a Presbyterian minister in New Brunswick, New Jersey. Gilbert was assisted in his preaching by other Presbyterians who, like himself, were educated for the ministry in the "Log College," founded in 1736 by Gilbert's father, William Tennent, Sr.

The revival spread to the Connecticut River Valley in 1734 and 1735 with the preaching of Jonathan Edwards. Edwards is regarded, even by secular scholars, as perhaps the greatest philosopher-theologian in American history. His sermons had an immense impact on those who heard them, despite the fact that they were often very long and always read from a manuscript. "Sinners in the Hands of an Angry God," first preached in 1741, is still read and often cited as an example of the Bible-based, Calvinist theology of the Great Awakening. John Wesley was the only leading figure of the revivals who was Arminian in his theology. It was his Arminianism that led John Wesley and George Whitefield in 1740 to agree to go their separate ways. All of the revivalists, however, stressed three things: the terror of the law to sinners, the unmerited grace of God, and the new birth in Jesus Christ.

By emphasizing a conversion experience and calling upon all to cast themselves upon the mercy of God, the preachers of the Great Awakening, sometimes by intent, democratized Calvinism by de-emphasizing the role of predestination. They also split the churches. The New England clergy split into "Old Lights" and "New Lights." The Old Lights were led by Charles Chauncy, who preached vigorously against the revival and against Edwards in particular. Edwards was the leader of the New Lights and supported the revival. The Old Lights evolved into the Unitarians in the early-nineteenth century. Presbyterians also split into "Old Side" and "New Side," but reunited in 1758. Even the Dutch Reformed and Baptists split temporarily in response to the revival.

Samuel Davies preached the revival among the Presbyterians in Virginia. Shubal Stearns and Daniel Marshall spread it to the Baptists in the southern colonies, where Devereux Jarratt, an Episcopalian, was instrumental in spreading a Methodist revivalism. George Whitefield made seven trips to the American colonies between 1738 and 1769. He preached outdoors to crowds numbered in the thousands. His close friend and supporter Benjamin Franklin estimated that thirty thousand people gathered in Philadelphia to hear Whitefield preach. Although Franklin was a great admirer of Whitefield—and even printed tracts and sermons for him—Franklin remained a Deist.

Whitefield was eloquent in both speech and manner. He preached to all classes, even to slaves, to whom most preachers would not preach. He founded an orphanage, wrote tracts for evangelizing the Native Americans, and influenced the founding of fifty colleges in America, including the College of New Jersey which later became Princeton University. Jonathan Edwards was appointed president of the college in 1758 and died later that year following a smallpox inoculation. George Whitefield died on September 30, 1770, of an asthma attack, having preached for two hours the previous day to a large crowd in inclement weather. John Wesley preached at his funeral.

The revivals of the late-seventeenth and eighteenth centuries had a profound impact on the history of the church. The modern Protestant foreign missionary movement can be traced directly to the influence of Zinzendorf and the Moravians. William Carey caught the vision, influencing the Baptists to send out missionaries. The Methodist mission movement began in 1786, when Thomas Coke was sent to India. In America, missions to the Native Americans were undertaken by David Brainerd and Jonathan Edwards.

The Sunday School movement was developed and popularized by the Anglican layman, Robert Raikes. Numerous colleges and other educational institutions were founded. Four of America's leading universities (Rutgers, Princeton, Dartmouth, and the University of Pennsylvania) came out of the Great Awakening.

As is always the case, the preaching of the gospel was accompanied by a passion for social justice. John Howard led the cause for prison reform. John Wesley established a free medical dispensary in 1746. A lending bank was also opened in 1746. One Methodist meeting house in London was turned into a workshop to provide jobs for the unemployed. The antislavery movement, begun in 1767, was a particular crusade that involved many evangelical leaders. John Newton (1725–1807), a former captain of a slave ship who became an Anglican minister after his conversion, was one of its best known leaders. The antislavery crusade was a particular cause for members of the Clapham Sect, a group of Christian politicians in England that included the famous abolitionist, William Wilberforce (1759–1833). In 1774, John Wesley published his *Thoughts on Slavery*. Just four days before his death, he wrote to Wilberforce urging him to continue the struggle in Parliament against slavery.

The Methodist revival in England is credited by historians with preventing England from experiencing a violent revolution in the eighteenth century such as happened in France (1789–1815). In America, the Great Awakening is said to have created a common identity among the thirteen diverse English colonies, and in so doing, contributed to the American Revolution. On the negative side of the ledger, by emphasizing individual conversion ("covenant of grace"), the idea of a "covenant people" shifted from the church to America and the American people. The Puritan mission of creating a Christian commonwealth (Geneva, Puritan England, New England) was transferred to the American colonists' struggle for "liberty" and eventually the new republic's idea of a "manifest destiny." Thus the Great Awakening unfortunately contributed to the rise of the cult of American civil religion.

TIMELINE FOR CHAPTER 7

1543	Nicolaus Copernicus's *On the Revolutions of the Celestial Spheres* (Heliocentric Theory)
1687	Isaac Newton's *Principia* (Mechanistic Universe)
1689	John Locke's *Essay Concerning Understanding* (Environmentalism)
1690	John Locke's *Two Treatises of Government* (Social Contract Theory)
1722	Herrnhut founded
1732	First Moravian missionaries sent out
1736	William Tennent, Sr., founds "Log Cabin College"
1738	John Wesley and George Whitefield preach revival in Bristol
1740–1745	War of Austrian Succession
1741	Jonathan Edwards preaches "Sinners in the Hands of an Angry God"
1748	David Hume's *An Enquiry Concerning Human Understanding* (Skepticism)
	Montesquieu's *The Spirit of the Laws* (Balance of Power Theory)
1751	Denis Diderot begins publication of the *Encyclopedia*
1756–1763	Seven Years' War
1772–1816	Francis Asbury and Methodist revival in America
1776	American Declaration of Independence
1789	French Revolution begins

WESTERN INTELLECTUAL HISTORY

c.1000–c.1700	*c. 1700–c.1900*	*c. 1900–Present*
Premodernity	Modernity	Postmodernity
Medieval View of Universe	Enlightenment Tradition	Enlightenment Tradition in Disarray
Christian Worldview	Secular Worldview	Secular Worldview
Order and Meaning for Humanity and the Universe	Order and Meaning for Humanity and the Universe	Chaos! No Meaning for Humanity or the Universe

CHAPTER EIGHT
The Church in a Modern World, 1789–1914: Part I

THE BIG PICTURE

Two great revolutions occurred during the nineteenth century that profoundly influenced the history of Christianity. They were the spread of industrialization throughout Europe and North America and a second scientific revolution that, together, resulted in the triumph of secularism. Both resulted from the spread of classical liberalism, which encouraged the spread of constitutional governments and *laissez faire* economics. For the Roman Catholic church, the clash with political liberalism meant the loss of the Papal States and the temporal power of the papacy. The papacy responded with a sweeping condemnation of everything "modern" and with efforts to strengthen the spiritual authority of the papacy within the Catholic Church. With the exception of the brief pontificate of Leo XIII, a conservative reaction prevailed throughout Catholicism. Within Protestantism, the challenge of secularism was answered by the outbreak of a Second Great Awakening during the first half of the century, followed by the appearance of well-organized evangelistic crusades during the second half of the century. Charles G. Finney represented the spirit of the Second Great Awakening, while D. L. Moody and C. H. Spurgeon characterized the new spirit of evangelistic revival that continued on through the twentieth century.

KEY EVENTS

1801	The appearance of an estimated twenty thousand people at a "camp meeting" revival at Cane Ridge, Kentucky marks the outbreak of the Second Great Awakening.
1835	The modern style of revivalism is born with the preaching of Charles G. Finney and the publication of his *Lectures on Revivalism* (1875).
1864	Pope Pius IX condemns all aspects of "modernism" in his *Syllabus of Errors*.
1869–1870	The Vatican Council establishes the doctrine of papal infallibility whenever the pope speaks *ex cathedra* on matters of faith or morals.
1873	The camp meeting revivals move indoors with the carefully-planned crusades of the evangelistic team of D. L. Moody and Ira D. Sankey.

The nineteenth century was a century of change and progress. An individual born in Europe or North America at the beginning of the century had a life expectancy of only thirty-five years. By 1900, life expectancy had risen to fifty years. The Western world of 1800 was still an agricultural world, dominated politically, socially, and economically by the landed aristocracy. During the course of the century, the Industrial Revolution spread across Europe and North America, completely transforming society. A new source of wealth from commerce and industry, rather than land, created a new class—the middle class—to challenge the dominance of the old, landed aristocracy.

The ideology of the middle class was classical liberalism, derived from the Enlightenment philosophers, especially John Locke and Adam Smith. The liberals wanted constitutional governments (preferably constitutional monarchies), with written constitutions and regular elections to representative assemblies. These institutions would protect the individual's inalienable rights and limit the authority of government to interfere with those rights. They did not desire democracy. For the middle-class liberal, natural rights were property rights. Those who did not possess property should not be allowed to exercise political power by either voting or holding public office.

The economic ideology of the middle class was capitalism, the *laissez faire* economic theory associated with Adam Smith. According to Smith, the government should not interfere in the economy (as was the case with eighteenth-century mercantilism), but rather allow the natural laws of the economy to operate freely. An "invisible hand," not the hand of God, but the selfish pursuit of individual gain, would guide the economy to a beneficial outcome for all. Such economic practice made possible the accumulation of great wealth but also resulted in the evils of early industrialization that at times made the institution of slavery on Southern plantations appear almost humane.

In the second half of the nineteenth century, the working class gained a class consciousness, and by the end of the century it was challenging the middle class's hold on political power in those nations that possessed constitutional governments. In Europe, where the churches were viewed as pillars of the established order, the working class abandoned religion. In America, where socialism never held much appeal for the working class, new denominations sprang up that targeted the laboring classes.

The rise of the working class paralleled the rise of a mass culture. By the turn of the twentieth century, the worst evils of the Industrial Revolution were overcome as workers gained the right to vote and to organize labor unions. The result was an increased standard of living, together with some disposable income and leisure time. These developments, in turn, encouraged the rise of a mass culture that was primarily working-class and secular in spirit.

Industrialization fostered what is sometimes called a Second Scientific Revolution during the second half of the nineteenth century. One aspect of this was a burst of technological innovations. There were so many new inventions that the head of the U.S. Patent Office in 1899 advised President William McKinley to abolish the office, because "everything that can be invented has been invented." Another aspect of the Second Scientific Revolution was a shift in the way people understood reality, that is, their worldview. This was due in no small part to the acceptance of Charles Darwin's theory of evolution.

Charles Darwin (1809–1882) first published his theory of evolution in 1859 in *On the Origin of Species* and then applied it specifically to humans in *The Descent of Man,* published in 1871. No longer did human beings see themselves as distinct creatures, created in the image of God. Instead, they were merely a higher form of animal life—higher because they possessed the ability to reason. Indeed, the Bible and the very idea of God were now seen as the evolutionary products of humanity's evolving religious consciousness. By the 1880s, the German philosopher Friedrich Nietzsche (1844–1900) concluded that the very idea of God was no longer believable. God, he said, was dead! Without God, or at least the idea of God, humanity had to face the idea of meaninglessness. Enlightenment scepticism had reached its logical conclusion—there is no clock maker.

The churches responded to the challenges of the nineteenth century in different ways. Because the Catholic church was so closely associated with the old order in Europe, it was a particular target of the revolutionary liberal forces that tried to destroy its political and spiritual influence. In response, the Catholic church pulled up the drawbridge, spending the nineteenth century strengthening the spiritual authority of the pope within the institutional church.

Protestants fared somewhat better. A Second Great Awakening in America and an evangelical revival in Great Britain and Europe inspired a host of volunteer associations that fought the evils of slavery and industrial exploitation. The nineteenth century was also the great century of Protestant foreign missions. By the turn of the twentieth century, however, the fortunes of Protestantism were beginning to wane as theological modernism made rapid progress. Bible-believing evangelicals embraced new theologies that emphasized evangelism, while abandoning the effort to transform society and its culture. The responsibility to actively pursue a just society, the only political mandate that

Christians can legitimately claim, was left to "liberal" Christians. Only during the 1970s did evangelicals rediscover their social conscience, and then only reluctantly in the face of the mounting abortion holocaust and the surge of neo-paganism.

CATHOLICISM
. . . .

The antireligious, anti-Christian bias of the French Enlightenment surfaced with a vengeance during the French Revolution. Voltaire had said, "Wipe out that infamous thing," referring specifically to the Catholic church that had given its blessing to the Old Order. In August 1789, the French National Assembly abolished the nation's compulsory church tithe. In November, it confiscated the church's property. Then on July 12, 1790, came the Civil Constitution of the Clergy, effectively subordinating the Catholic church to the state. The number of bishops was reduced by almost half. The clergy, bishops, and priests were to be elected by the people and required to take an oath of loyalty to the Revolution. Pope Pius VI (1775–1799) responded by declaring the Civil Constitution of the Clergy heretical and by suspending all clergy who took the required oath.

The revolutionary government's response to the pope's condemnation increased the spirit of anticlericalism spreading across France. Many clergy, perhaps as many as forty thousand, were jailed. Some were executed in a spectacle called "de-Christianization by immersion." They were tied together in pairs and tossed into the river, reminiscent of the manner in which Anabaptists were executed in the sixteenth century. In its most radical phase, the Revolution tried to outlaw Christianity altogether and put in its place the "Cult of Reason." Deceased heroes of the Enlightenment and Revolution were granted sainthood. On November 10, 1794, Demoiselle Candeille, an actress from the Paris Opera, was carried into the Notre-Dame Cathedral in Paris as the personification of the Goddess of Reason.

The Cult of Reason was too extreme even for Maximilien Robespierre, the architect of the "Reign of Terror." He halted the anti-Christian campaign, because it was alienating too many people. In June 1794, Robespierre introduced the "Worship of the Supreme Being," an institutionalized version of Deism. This too failed. After Napoleon Bonaparte (1769–1821) came to power in 1799, he made peace with the Catholic Church by signing the Concordat of 1801 with Pope Pius VI. The Concordat of 1801, which remained in force until 1905, recognized Catholicism as "the religion of the great majority of the French citizens," but did not restore its property. The French clergy were thereafter paid by the government. The papacy, in turn, recognized the legitimacy of the French state.

Napoleon was not a religious man, but he recognized the importance of religious belief as a foundation for order in society. He once commented, "Men who do not believe in God—one does not govern them, one shoots them."[31] In February 1808, French troops occupied Rome. In 1809, Napoleon annexed the Papal States. When Pius VII (1800–1823) responded by excommunicating Napoleon, Pius was exiled to Fontainebleau, near Paris, where he remained until 1814. Not surprisingly, the papacy emerged from its experience with the French Revolution with a spirit of uncompromising hostility towards liberalism and all that followed from it, including democracy, tolerance, and all things modern.

Napoleon was finally defeated in 1815 by the united forces of Great Britain, Prussia, Austria, and Russia. The conservative victors met at Vienna to draft a peace settlement and attempt to restore the old pre-Revolution order in Europe. Until the middle of the century, the forces of liberalism and nationalism were suppressed. Political conservatism and cultural romanticism held sway from 1815 to 1848, creating a favorable environment for the Catholic church. Upon his return to Rome in 1814, Pope Pius VII issued a papal bull restoring the Inquisition, the *Index,* and the Jesuits. Restrictions on Catholics were removed in Britain in 1829 and on the European continent in Austria, France, and Prussia by mid-century.

[31]Quoted in Robert B. Holtman, *The Napoleonic Revolution* (Philadelphia: Lippincott, 1967), 121.

The Oxford Movement within the Anglican church helped the Catholic church in Britain. The Oxford (or Anglo-Catholic) Movement within the Anglican church emphasized apostolic succession, baptismal regeneration, and ritual. In 1845, the two most prominent leaders of the movement, John Henry Newman and Henry Edward Manning, joined the Catholic church. More than two hundred Anglican clergy and professors from Cambridge and Oxford universities followed their lead.

In 1846, the progressive-minded Italian patriot, Cardinal Mastai-Ferretti, was elected Pope Pius IX (1846–1878). Conservatives everywhere were alarmed at the prospect of a liberal pope. Pius IX proclaimed an amnesty in the Papal States, pardoning all political prisoners. In Rome, the Jews were allowed to leave their ghetto. A Council of State was established that many interpreted as a step towards constitutional government. But Pius IX's liberal phase came to an abrupt end with the liberal revolutions that swept through Europe's capitals in 1848. When revolution broke out in Rome, and a liberal republic was proclaimed, Pius IX was forced to flee. He did not return to Rome until 1850, and then with the support of a French army.

The events of 1848–1850 cleansed Pius IX of any remaining liberal sympathies. When he returned to Rome, he was determined to strengthen the spiritual authority of the papacy. In 1854, he issued a papal bull, *Ineffabilis Deus,* which established as dogma the belief that Mary was conceived without "any taint of original sin." In 1864, Pius IX issued the papal encyclical *Quanta Cura,* which contained the *Syllabus of Errors.* The latter contained a sweeping condemnation of the modern world. Among the eighty errors of modernism that the faithful were required to reject were religious toleration, secular education, Bible distribution societies (termed "daring heralds of infidelity and heresy"), freedom of speech, civil marriage, the view that the pope did not possess temporal power, and modern philosophies including socialism, communism, liberalism, rationalism, and naturalism. The *Syllabus of Errors* came on the heels of Pius IX's reaffirmation of Boniface

VIII's assertion in *Unam Sanctum* (1301) that there is no salvation outside the Roman Catholic church.

In March 1861, Italian unification was achieved with Victor Emmanuel as king. The Papal States were incorporated into the Kingdom of Italy, except for Rome, which had been protected by a garrison of French soldiers since 1850. In September 1870, following the defeat of France in the Franco-Prussian War, Rome became the capital of Italy. Pius IX retreated to the Vatican, from which he and his successors conducted "war" against the Italian state. Finally, in 1929, the Lateran Treaty between Benito Mussolini and Pius XI (1922–1939) was signed, creating the Vatican City as a sovereign state under the temporal rule of the pope.

Meanwhile, Pius IX convened the Vatican Council that sat from December 8, 1869, until July 18, 1870. The carefully orchestrated council reaffirmed papal supremacy, issuing a declaration on papal infallibility. The declaration, passed by a vote of 533 to 2, declared that whenever the pope speaks on matters of faith or morals in his capacity as supreme head of the church on earth (*ex cathedra*), he cannot err. Those proclamations that are made *ex cathedra* do not require prior consent of the church.

The proclamation of papal infallibility resulted in an intensification of anticlericalism, especially in Germany and France. In Germany, Otto von Bismarck, the "Iron Chancellor," launched what became known as the *Kulturkampf*, or "culture war," against what he called the "Black Internationale" (the Catholic church). It lasted from 1872 to 1878. The Jesuits were expelled from Germany in 1872. In 1873, a series of anti-Catholic laws (the "Falk," or "May Laws") were passed by the Reichstag. They secularized education, required civil marriage, closed the Catholic Office in the Ministry of Religion, and required Catholic clergy to study at state universities.

This persecution merely strengthened the Catholic church in Germany. Many bishops and priests chose prison rather than capitulation, thus becoming martyrs. The Catholic Center Party strengthened its position in the Reichstag. By 1878, Bismarck saw the rapid rise of the Social Democratic Party, the leading

Marxist-based workers' party, as a greater threat to the state than Catholicism. When the more conciliatory Leo XIII (1878–1903) ascended the papal throne in 1878, Bismarck quietly abandoned the *Kulturkampf,* seeking support from the Catholic Center Party for his crusade against the "Red Internationale" of the Social Democratic Party.

In France, Catholics found themselves at odds with the Third Republic, founded in 1870. Until 1892, French Catholics favored restoration of the monarchy. The Republic responded by passing a number of anticlerical laws that required all religious organizations to register with the state. These laws also legalized divorce and banned religious teaching in the public schools. Between 1901 and 1904, nearly fourteen thousand Christian schools were closed in France. In 1905, the Separation Law, introduced by the socialist premier Aristide Briand, passed—canceling the Concordat of 1801. All state support of the Catholic church ended and all church buildings became state property. Complete freedom of religion was proclaimed as the Third Republic sought to define itself as a secular state.

The pontificate of Leo XIII was a brief, liberal interlude in the steady conservative direction of the Catholic church. Leo XIII encouraged Bible study and called for justice for the working class in his social encyclical *Rerum Novarum* (1890). The encyclical was influenced by the movement known as Social Catholicism—a movement developed particularly in Germany from the 1830s onward. In many ways, the leaders of Social Catholicism were similar to the Protestants in Great Britain and the United States who fought against slavery and for factory legislation to end the exploitation of children and women in the factories and the mines. Among the best known leaders of Social Catholicism were the Freiburg social scientist, Josef Ritter von Buss, the Catholic labor movement leader, Franz Hitze, and most importantly, the Bishop of Mainz, Wilhelm Emanuel Freiherr von Ketteler. Ketteler and other Social Catholics believed they could find an alternative to both socialism and capitalism in the works of Thomas Aquinas. It would be a society in which people recognized that they "enjoyed not an absolute and unconditional ownership of property, but only the right to use property in accordance with divine law."[32]

With the death of Leo XIII and the election of Pius X (1903–1914), the Catholic church returned to its conservative course. Pius X broke off diplomatic relations with France in 1904. At the same time, he tried to strengthen the authority of the church in the lives of the faithful. In 1904, he revived the use of the Gregorian chant and encouraged the veneration of the Virgin Mary. On the whole, the Catholic church lost virtually all of its temporal power during the nineteenth century, but did succeed in strengthening its spiritual authority among Catholics.

A NEW AWAKENING

The Great Awakening (1725–1760) in America was a major influence in creating a common identity among the thirteen diverse English colonies. This in turn contributed to their success in the Revolution. By the time the colonies achieved independence from Great Britain, the influence of the Great Awakening was largely past. Deism held more sway than Christianity—especially among the educated elite. The influence of the churches was at an all-time low, as church attendance dropped to only 5 to 10 percent of the adult population. The tide began to turn in 1787, however, when revivals broke out at Hampton-Sydney College and Washington College, two Presbyterian schools in Virginia. In 1802, revival broke out at Yale College, where Timothy Dwight, Jonathan Edwards' grandson, had become president in 1795. From Yale, the revival spread to other New England colleges.

Revival came to the American frontier with the preaching of James McGready, a bold and uncompromising Presbyterian. McGready's zeal for revival was kindled by a visit to Hampton-Sydney College. After a brief stint in North Carolina,

---

[32]Thomas Parker Moon, *The Labor Problem and Social Catholic Movement in France* (New York, 1921), 122.

he moved to Kentucky in 1789. David Rice, the first minister to settle along the Kentucky frontier in 1783, commented that there was scarcely a man or woman with a "creditable profession of religion," or any knowledge of "the first principles of religion."[33] By all accounts, McGready was one of God's gifted orators in the tradition of St. Bernard of Clairvaux and Jonathan Edwards. When he spoke, he painted word pictures of heaven so beautiful that his rough and often lawless congregation longed to be there. His portrayal of the horrors of hell was so vivid that they trembled in fear. Convicted sinners would fall on the floor weeping and pleading, "What shall I do to be saved?"[34] It was a response similar to what occurred when Jonathan Edwards would preach "Sinners in the Hands of an Angry God."

After a successful revival at Red River in 1800, McGready sent word ahead that he would preach at the Gasper River church in July. The news spread along the frontier. Families and individuals came from as much as a hundred miles away—by foot, by wagon, by whatever means available. They brought with them tents and food so that they could camp out for the length of the service. This first "camp meeting" lasted for several days. The best known of the early frontier camp meetings occurred at Cane Ridge, Kentucky, in August 1801.

According to some accounts, as many as twenty thousand people attended the Cane Ridge camp meeting. In descriptions of the meeting by friends and foes alike, there is mention (perhaps exaggerated) of strange "signs" manifesting themselves. Participants were said to have leaped with joy when saved. There were reports of jerking, barking, dancing, and rolling on the ground. The Presbyterian General Assembly of 1805 was alarmed by such reports and tried to dampen the revival, attributing the "excesses" to the influence of the Methodist doctrine of grace. The result was a split, as the pro-revivalist Cumberland Presbyterians left the Kentucky Synod. The Second Great Awak-

---

[33]Quoted in Thomas A. Askew and Peter W. Spellman, *The Churches and the American Experience: Ideals and Institutions* (Grand Rapids: Baker Book House, 1984), 77.
[34]Ibid., 78.

ening began with the Presbyterians, but it was carried over the mountains by the Baptists and Methodists.

Two contrasting movements were influenced by the Second Great Awakening: Unitarianism and revivalism. Unitarianism, a religious movement that believes in the goodness of humanity and rejects the Trinity and biblical revelation, can be traced back to the Radical Reformation in the sixteenth century. The first organized Unitarian congregation in Great Britain was Essex Chapel, London, in 1774. In early America, many prominent Americans, including Thomas Jefferson, held Unitarian views. The First Unitarian church in America was King's Chapel in Boston. In 1805, King's Chapel, the oldest Episcopal church in America, rejected the doctrine of the Trinity and declared itself Unitarian. Also in 1805, Henry Ware, a Unitarian, was appointed to a theological chair at Harvard University. William Ellery Channing, pastor of the Federal Street Congregational Church in Boston, developed Unitarian doctrine and was instrumental in the founding of the American Unitarian Association in 1825. By then, there were over one hundred Unitarian churches in New England.

As we mentioned earlier, revivalism was another movement that came out of the Second Great Awakening in America, and its effects were far-reaching. In a sense, Charles G. Finney, Dwight L. Moody, Billy Sunday, Billy Graham, and countless other evangelists and revivalists are heirs of James McGready and the Second Great Awakening. The ongoing appeal of revivalism comes in part from the Arminian doctrine that God has an offer of salvation available to all mankind at all times, and the individual can come to Christ if only he or she will choose to accept that offer. In the history of revivalism, no figure is more important than Charles Grandison Finney (1792–1875).

Charles G. Finney was converted in 1821 as a result of his personal study of the Bible. Believing that his conversion included "a retainer from the Lord to plead his cause,"[35] Finney abandoned the practice of law to begin preaching in 1824. Also

[35] Quoted in J. D. Douglas, General Editor, *The New International Dictionary of the Christian Church* (Grand Rapids: Zondervan Publishing House, 1978), 376.

in 1824, Finney was ordained by the St. Lawrence Presbytery, despite his belief that atonement was for all, rather than just the elect. He pastored Second Presbyterian Church in New York City, before setting out to preach revivals in Ohio, Pennsylvania, and New England. With Finney, the revivals moved from outdoor camp meetings to large, urban, indoor auditoriums.

Many of the standard features of modern revivalism were first introduced by Finney, including protracted meetings, the altar call, special music, the "anxious bench," using "you" when referring to sinners, holding prayer meetings at "unreasonable hours," and allowing women to pray and speak. Critics then and now have accused Finney of manipulating his listeners, a charge Finney seems to add credit to in his book, *Lectures on Revivalism* (1835). There, he clearly states his belief that "a revival is not a miracle, or dependent on a miracle in any sense. It is a purely philosophical [i.e., scientific] result of the right use of the constituted means."[36] "Finneyism" has become a derogatory term applied to many modern revivalists and televangelists to distinguish their manipulative tactics and results from those true revivals that are a work of God.

In 1835, Finney joined the faculty of Oberlin College in Ohio and served as the college's president from 1851–1866. During that time, he became a major force in linking the Second Great Awakening in America with social reform—including abolition of slavery and women's rights. Antoinette (Brown) Blackwell, the first woman to be ordained in the United States (1835), received her theological education at Oberlin College. African-Americans were also admitted to Oberlin under Finney's leadership.

Revivals became a staple of American religious life through the end of the nineteenth century and into the twentieth century. An interdenominational prayer meeting in New York City on September 23, 1857, grew from six people to ten thousand people in prayer meetings scattered throughout the city. During the Civil War, revival broke out among the Confederate soldiers in 1863 and 1864. Perhaps as many as one hundred thousand were converted.

[36] Quoted in Askew and Spellman, *Churches and the American Experience,* 82.

Two individuals stand out as exemplifying the evangelistic spirit of the church during the second half of the nineteenth century—D. L. Moody and C. H. Spurgeon. Dwight Lyman Moody (1837–1899) was a simple layman without any formal theological training. His significance in shaping mass evangelism, however, rivals that of Charles G. Finney. One of nine children in a Unitarian family, his mother was widowed when he was only four years old. At thirteen, Moody left school, and at seventeen he went to work as a shoe salesman in his uncle's shoe store. Led to the Lord by a Sunday school teacher, Moody was denied membership in the local church when he first applied, because he lacked sufficient knowledge of Christian doctrine.

In 1856, Moody moved to Chicago, where he soon became engrossed in promoting the Chicago YMCA and a host of other urban ministries. His introduction to mass evangelism came while visiting London, England, when he was asked to be a substitute preacher. The impressive response to his closing invitation got him invited to return to Britain in 1873 for a two-year evangelistic campaign. Meanwhile, Moody teamed up with Ira D. Sankey. Sankey was a musician and Civil War veteran, who sang in a rich baritone voice while accompanying himself on a small reed organ. Together, they presented the gospel in word and song to an estimated three million listeners across Britain during the two-year crusade. After their return to the United States, Moody and Sankey spent the next five years holding crusades across America from Brooklyn to San Francisco. The evangelistic team of Moody and Sankey remained together for more than a quarter century, leading countless souls to salvation through faith in Jesus Christ.

D. L. Moody set a standard and style that influenced many evangelists who followed after him, such as Billy Graham. With Moody, the evangelistic crusade not only moved indoors, it also left behind the roughness and spontaneity of the camp meeting. His crusades were carefully planned in advance. Every detail—from promotion to follow up—was taken care of before Moody and Sankey arrived in town. Moody himself appeared neatly dressed, like a businessman. He spoke in a calm and plain voice. His goal was to see sinners saved, and his message was always a simple one (the same one preached by the early church): the promise of salvation and eternal life by grace through faith in Jesus Christ. There were no theological arguments or sermons on the fine points of Christian doctrine. Rather, Moody presented the gospel in a clear and simple language that his hearers could understand. The spontaneous outbursts that characterized the old-fashioned camp meetings were discouraged. Moody did not hesitate to halt his sermon long enough to ask ushers to escort overly enthusiastic individuals from the auditorium.

D. L. Moody set a high standard in another area that, sadly, has been too often ignored by those who came after him in the twentieth century. Moody relied heavily on financial support from wealthy patrons like Marshall Field, Cornelius Vanderbilt II, and J. P. Morgan. Although one might question the motives behind the generosity of such tycoons (some of whom are referred to by historians as "Robber Barons"), Moody, himself, remained above reproach. He raised enormous sums during his lifetime, not only to support his crusades, but to finance several schools and seminaries, including Moody Bible Institute. Yet, when Moody died in 1899, his entire estate consisted of only five hundred dollars. Not even that small sum would have been left, except for the fact that he did not know of its existence.

If D. L. Moody had a counterpart in Britain, it was Charles Haddon Spurgeon (1834–1892), the "prince of the preachers." The son and grandson of Independent pastors, Spurgeon was converted at age sixteen. During the winter of 1850, he wandered into the Artillery Street Primitive Methodist Chapel in Colchester, Essex, to escape the cold. There he found salvation, and surrendered his life to serving the Lord. In that same year, he became a Baptist and preached his first sermon. After a brief ministry at Waterbeach, Cambridgeshire, Spurgeon was called to pastor New Park Street Chapel in Southwark, London. Soon the building could no longer hold those who wished to hear Spurgeon. In 1859,

New Park Street Chapel became the new Metropolitan Tabernacle, with seating to accommodate six thousand hearers.

Unlike Moody, Spurgeon did not travel and hold crusades. He did, however, support Moody's crusades in Britain. Spurgeon was an evangelical Calvinist, who actively opposed both hyper-Calvinism and Arminianism. He struggled against the spread of liberal theology in the Baptist Union. Finally, in 1874, Spurgeon withdrew from the liberal Baptist Union but refused to help found a new denomination. Like Moody, Spurgeon's ministry expanded beyond preaching to include the founding of an orphanage and Spurgeon's College. Also, he found time to publish several books, edit a monthly magazine, and publish his sermons each week. His collected sermons fill more than fifty published volumes. No other preacher of Spurgeon's time achieved his level of popularity.

Another movement in the church that gained momentum during this time was the so-called "holiness movement." The holiness movement had its roots in John Wesley's teaching on entire sanctification and Christian perfection. It was instantaneous and emotional, a kind of "second blessing," or "baptism of the Holy Spirit." The movement came into its own in the late 1860s with the founding of the National Camp Meeting Association for the Promotion of Holiness. The holiness movement spawned a host of new denominations, including the Free Methodists, Wesleyan Methodists, the Church of the Nazarene, and the Church of God. Other denominations like the Christian and Missionary Alliance and organizations like the Salvation Army were influenced by, but not a part of, the holiness movement.

The American holiness movement had its counterpart in Britain in the "Keswick," or "Oxford Movement," begun in 1875. The Keswick movement, which continues today, was more influenced by Reformed than Arminian theology. It rejected perfectionism, emphasizing instead the "fullness of the Spirit" and "practical holiness." Again, it was a second blessing, or filling of the Holy Spirit, that had to be sought after. Once received, it empowered the individual to live a victorious life. The movement's influence was widespread. Moody brought it back to America in 1875. It was a key influence in the German Fellowship Movement (1880–1910) and the great Welsh revival of 1905.

Another offspring of the holiness movement was Pentecostalism, with its emphasis on "baptism in the Holy Spirit" and the charismatic "gifts of the Spirit." Pentecostalism began in 1901 at Bethel College, a Bible school in Topeka, Kansas, where a former Methodist minister, Charles F. Parkam (1873–1929), taught the students using the Bible as his only textbook. Within a decade, the movement which emphasized the "gift of speaking in tongues" as a sign of baptism by the Holy Spirit spread around the world.

Camp meetings and evangelistic crusades were but two means by which the gospel was spread during the nineteenth century. Foreign missions was another, and the very practical work of devoted believers ministering to the needs of the poor and working for social justice was yet another. The linking of spiritual renewal and social reform has always been a characteristic of authentic revival.

The further advance of the church in the nineteenth century was, however, threatened by the advance of secularism. Darwinian evolution became an underlying assumption of the natural and social sciences by the end of the century. Christian seminaries were not immune to its influence, and many sought compromise by embracing theistic evolution. They were encouraged in their retreat from biblical authority by the growth of higher criticism in biblical scholarship and the spread of liberal theology.

TIMELINE FOR CHAPTER 8

1789	The French Revolution begins
1790	Civil Constitution of the Clergy
1794	Worship of the Supreme Being is introduced in France
1799	The Second Great Awakening begins in America
1801	Concordat of 180
	Cane Ridge Kentucky Camp Meeting
1814–1815	The Defeat of Napoleon and the Congress of Vienna
1825	American Unitarian Association is founded

1835	Charles G. Finney publishes *Lectures on Revivalism*
1848	Revolutions of 1848 in Europe
1850	Charles H. Spurgeon opens the Metropolitan Tabernacle
1856	Dwight L. Moody moves to Chicago
1861–1865	The American Civil War
1864	Pius IX issues *Syllabus of Errors*
1869–1870	Vatican (I) Council
1872–1878	*Kulturkampf* in Germany
1890	Leo XIII issues *Rerum Novarum*

MODERN ECUMENICAL COUNCILS (Roman Catholic)

Council of Trent (1545–1563) — *Called by Pope Paul III* — Reaffirmed medieval church doctrine, while rejecting the teaching of the Protestant Reformation. The Vulgate is declared the official translation of the church; the number of sacraments is set at seven; the Bible and church tradition are affirmed as authoritative; and transubstantiation is affirmed.

First Vatican Council (1869–1870) — *Called by Pope Pius IX* — Doctrine of papal infallibility (when the pope speaks *ex cathedra* on matters of faith and morals) is promulgated.

Second Vatican Council (1962–1965) — *Called by Pope John XXIII* — An update of the church, requiring Mass to be delivered in vernacular language with participation of the laity, encouraging Bible translation and reading, encouraging dialogue with other faiths (Protestants), and affirming freedom of religion. Also, the council ended the publication of the *Index of Prohibited Books,* affirmed the veneration of the Virgin Mary, and affirmed that the Roman Catholic church is the only means of salvation.

CHAPTER NINE

The Church in a Modern World, 1789–1914: Part II

THE BIG PICTURE

A passion for both spiritual renewal and social reform characterized the revivalists of the Second Great Awakening in America and the evangelicals in Great Britain. In America during the first half of the eighteenth century, a whole host of reform movements (societies), known collectively as the "Benevolent Empire," came out of the Second Great Awakening. Chief among these reform movements was the struggle for temperance and the abolition of slavery. In Britain, William Wilberforce led the parliamentary battle to end slavery in the British Empire, and Lord Ashley led the parliamentary struggle to alleviate the evils of industrialization. Much of the zeal for social reform among Christians, especially in America, waned in the second half of the century as evangelicals increasingly emphasized evangelism, while becoming passive on social issues. The cause of justice in modern society was taken up by the theologically liberal advocates of the Social Gospel. Although evangelicals abdicated an important part of the gospel to the liberals, they enthusiastically pursued foreign missions. The nineteenth century was the great century of Protestant missions. Evangelical men and women from America and Europe (especially Britain) founded foreign mission societies, independent faith missions, and went in increasing numbers to foreign lands. There, they often restored the link between spirirtual renewal and reform.

KEY EVENTS

1792   William Carey goes to India as a "tent-making" missionary, inaugurating the movement that would dub the nineteenth century "the great century of Protestant foreign missions."

1823   William Wilberforce and other members of the Clapham Sect found the British and Foreign Anti-Slavery Society to agitate for the abolition of slavery in the British Empire.

1834   The "Lane Rebels," a group of seminary students, establish Oberlin College, which quickly becomes a center for abolitionist and other social reform causes prior to the Civil War.

1880s   Theological liberalism arrives from Germany and soon begins its rapid advance among American seminaries and churches.

When William Wilberforce (1759–1833) was only a boy at Hull Grammar School, the headmaster's brother, Isaac Milner, would lift young William onto a table so that the teachers at the school could listen to him read. Wilberforce had a beautiful voice as a child and grew up to become one of the greatest orators in the history of Parliament. Small of stature, it was said that the shrimp grew into a whale when he began to speak. Although Wilberforce hated evil, he loved everyone he met. Even his political opponents admired the one whom they called "the nightingale of the House of Commons."

Wilberforce was converted in 1784 while accompanying Isaac Milner on a trip to France. It was either his reading of the New Testament, or, as some sources report, his reading of Philip Doddridge's classic, *The Rise and Progress of Religion in the Soul* (1745), that led to his conversion. In 1780, Wilberforce was elected to Parliament, where he served until his retirement in 1825. As a member of Parliament, Wilberforce was an ally of William Pitt the Younger, the youngest prime minister ever. It was Pitt who persuaded him to remain in Parliament after his conversion, arguing that it was his Christian duty to do so. Even before his conversion, Wilberforce championed parliamentary reform, political emancipation for Roman Catholics, and the abolition of slavery. In 1786, Wilberforce announced his belief that God had called him to two great tasks, "the suppression of the slave trade and the reformation of manners."[37]

The struggle against the slave trade became the great cause of Wilberforce's life. His first volley in the war against slavery came in the form of an essay on the evils of the slave trade, written when he was only fourteen. In 1779, John Newton, a former slave trader turned Anglican clergyman and antislavery crusader, preached a series of sermons in London on Handel's *Messiah.* Wilberforce journeyed to London and sought out Newton—presumably to learn firsthand about the evils of the slave trade. Newton, who gave his testimony in the hymn "Amazing Grace," knew what it meant for God to place upon one's heart a burden such as the cause of justice in a fallen world. He had spent his early life profiting from evil until God's amazing grace taught his heart to fear and opened his eyes to see. From that time on, Newton devoted his life to abolishing the evil that once was his livelihood.

Wilberforce became the center of a group of wealthy Anglican evangelicals who were committed to the cause of social improvement—especially the abolition of slavery. Originally known as "the Saints," the group became known as the "Clapham Sect," named after the community and parish where most members resided. The Clapham evangelicals regularly spent three hours a day in prayer. When key issues were up for parliamentary debate, they organized prayer support across England. When necessary, they rallied popular support behind a boycott of slave-produced goods.

Hannah More, regarded as the leading female literary figure in England at the time, was encouraged by Wilberforce and Newton to devote her talents to the cause of social reform. With financial support from Clapham members, she set up Sunday schools and schools to teach the poor such industrial skills as spinning. She employed her literary talents to write 114 religious tracts (the

---

[37]Quoted in Richard F. Lovelace, *Dynamics of Spiritual Life: An Evangelical Theology of Renewal* (Exeter, England: Paternoster Press, 1979), 370.

Cheap Repository Tracts) aimed at the lower classes. Publication of the tracts was financed by Wilberforce and Henry Thornton, a wealthy banker and member of the Clapham sect. While Hannah More spoke to the poor, Wilberforce tried to spread the group's evangelical views among the upper classes through his popular book, *Practical View of the Prevailing Religious System of Professed Christians in the Higher and Middle Classes in this Country Contrasted with Real Christianity* (1797). The Clapham members were instrumental in the founding of the Church Missionary Society (1799), the British and Foreign Bible Society (1804), and in getting Parliament in 1813 to permit missionaries to go to India. They were active in a wide variety of causes, but none so much as the struggle against slavery.

Wilberforce was joined in the struggle against slavery by Granville Sharp and Thomas Clarkson, fellow members of the Clapham Sect. Together they devoted their careers and their fortunes to the struggle. Granville Sharp won a court decision in 1772, banning slavery in England. Thomas Clarkson gathered the data used by Wilberforce in parliamentary debates. With the support of others they made steady progress. In 1787, they founded the colony of Sierra Leone as a refuge for freed slaves who wished to return to Africa. The colony was supported financially by members of the Clapham Sect. One member, Zachary Macaulay, served as governor of the colony from 1793 to 1799, and then as secretary of the Sierra Leone Company until the British Crown assumed control in 1808.

On March 25, 1807, Parliament abolished the slave trade in the British West Indies. In 1825, Wilberforce retired from the House of Commons, turning the leadership of the struggle for abolition of slavery over to Thomas Fowell Buxton. Buxton helped found the British and Foreign Anti-Slavery Society in 1823. Slavery was finally abolished by act of Parliament in 1833, just one month after William Wilberforce's death.

Although Wilberforce and his friends in the Clapham Sect concentrated their energies on the struggle against slavery, they did not ignore the evils of industrialization at home. They were among the first to speak out against the "white slavery" that forced children as young as four and five years of age to labor underground in the mines. These children often worked six days a week from sunup to sundown, and were tied to machines in factories and whipped with leather straps to keep them awake during the twelve to fourteen hours of daily labor. The Clapham Sect was appalled by the practice of strapping women, some of them pregnant, to coal cars as if they were donkeys and forcing them to pull the cars through the mine tunnels on their hands and knees. The struggle for justice for the working classes of industrial England was, however, more fully taken up by a second generation of evangelical reformers. Among them, Anthony Ashley Cooper, the Seventh Earl of Shaftesbury (1801–1885), stands out.

Shaftesbury, or "Lord Ashley," as he was known, was a descendent of his namesake, the famous Deist and Third Earl of Shaftesbury, who is credited with having exported English Deism to Germany through his writings. His mother was a socialite, and his father an alcoholic politician. He was led to the Lord by his nanny. At age fourteen, he dedicated his life to serving the poor, a commitment from which he never wavered. He became the undisputed leader of the evangelicals within the Anglican church and the most effective reformer in nineteenth-century England.

Like Wilberforce and other evangelical reformers before him, Shaftesbury drew strength from a daily dependence on the Lord. Asked by his son how he could sustain so much effort in so many directions for so long, Shaftesbury replied, "By hearty prayer to Almighty God before I begin, by entering into it with faith and zeal, and by making my end His glory and the good of mankind."[38] He was driven by the belief that every human being was the image-bearer of God and therefore entitled to a life of dignity. It is not too much to say that Shaftesbury, like Mother Teresa (1910–1997), saw in serving the poor—the least in the kingdom of God—an opportunity to serve Christ, himself. Speaking at a Social Service Congress in Liverpool in 1859, Shaftesbury echoed the Old Testament prophets when he

---

[38] Quoted in Lovelace, *Dynamics of Evangelical Renewal,* 381-382.

observed that the gospel of salvation cannot rightly be separated from the cause of justice:

> When people say we should think more of the soul and less of the body, my answer is that the same God who made the soul made the body also. . . . I maintain that God is worshiped not only by the spiritual but by the material creation. Our bodies, the temples of the Holy Ghost, ought not to be corrupted by preventable disease, degraded by avoidable filth, and disabled for his service by unnecessary suffering.[39]

During his six decades in Parliament, Shaftesbury was responsible for an impressive array of legislation on behalf of the laboring poor. The Factory Act of 1833 limited the labor of children. The Mines Act of 1842 took women and girls out of the mines and forbid the employment of boys under thirteen. Shaftesbury secured creation of the Royal Commission of Inquiry to investigate the employment of children. Between 1864 and 1867, Parliament passed legislation to regulate the employment of women and children in industry. One of his major achievements was passage of the Climbing Boys Act in 1875, which addressed the horrible exploitation of small boys as chimney sweeps. In addition to his work in Parliament, Shaftesbury served as president of the Ragged Schools Union for thirty-nine years and served in other official roles on numerous missionary societies and organizations that aimed at reforming society and spreading the gospel. "When I feel old age creeping upon me," he once said, "and know that I must soon die . . . I cannot bear to leave this world with all the misery in it."[40] When he died in 1885, misery was not ended—but there was less. Shaftesbury, like so many Christians of that era in church history, believed that those who had experienced spiritual revival in their own lives just naturally became active in helping the less fortunate.

[39] Quoted in *Eerdmans' Handbook to the History of Christianity*, 519.
[40] Quoted in Lovelace, *Dynamics of Spiritual Life*, 410.

Similarly, the revivals that moved across continental Europe during the nineteenth century generated volunteer societies that founded orphanages, homes for the elderly, and urban missions. In Germany, Johann H. Wichern founded the Innere Mission, which he hoped would bring together the preaching of the gospel and practical social reform. One concrete expression of his vision was the establishment of "Rough House," a school for neglected children near Hamburg. The Dutch historian and statesman, Guillaume Groen van Prinsterer, worked to promote Christian education in the Netherlands. Prinsterer influenced Abraham Kuyper, the renowned Calvinist theologian and political activist, who founded the Free University of Amsterdam in 1880 and served briefly as prime minister of the Netherlands between 1901 and 1905.

CHRISTIANS AND REFORM IN AMERICA

In America, the Second Great Awakening led to the formation of a wide range of voluntary societies aimed at winning the world for Christ by the salvation of souls and the transformation of society. Reform societies sprang up to promote temperance, women's rights, foreign missions, educational and prison reform, and the abolition of slavery. With varying degrees of success, Christians aimed their efforts at the widespread neglect of the Sabbath, the overindulgence in alcoholic beverages, and the evils of dueling, gambling, and prostitution.

Intemperance was of particular concern, for alcoholism had reached epidemic proportions in the 1820s, when roughly three times as much distilled liquor was consumed as is today. The American Temperance Society was founded in 1826 by a group of clergymen, and a nationwide temperance campaign was launched. By 1834, there were five thousand local branches with a total membership of over one million. Their influence was significant. During the 1830s, consumption dropped by more than 50 percent.[41]

[41]Robert A. Divine, et. al., *America Past and Present,* vol. 1, *To 1877* (Glenview, IL: Scott Foresman and Company), 303.

The "Benevolent Empire," as the network of reform and missionary societies in America became known, was made up largely of northern evangelicals from the Congregationalist and Presbyterian camps. Among the leading figures were the two Tappan brothers, Arthur and Lewis. The Tappan brothers were wealthy New York merchants. Arthur was the nation's largest silk merchant, and Lewis was founder of what later became the Wall Street firm of Dun & Bradstreet, Inc. They lived a simple lifestyle, believing that they were only stewards of the wealth God had given them. They used their great wealth to fund the evangelistic campaigns of Charles G. Finney and a whole host of reform efforts—especially the abolition of slavery. The Tappan brothers are considered typical examples of nineteenth-century evangelical reformers in America. They also reflect some of the fundamental changes that were under way among evangelicals at the time.

Arthur and Lewis Tappan were the children of a Northhampton, Massachusetts mother, who was an unwavering follower of Jonathan Edwards. In fact, they lived for a while in Edwards' old home. The brothers were influenced by the preaching of William Ellery Channing, the Unitarian pastor of Federal Street Congregational Church in Boston. Lewis became a Unitarian briefly and even served as treasurer of the American Unitarian Association founded by Channing in 1825. In 1828, however, he returned to the Calvinist faith in which he was reared. The "new" Calvinism of Lewis Tappan and other evangelical reformers of the period was one, according to biographer William Wyatt-Brown, in which God was "concerned with the happiness of mankind, the growth of the visible Church, the extinction of heresy, and the establishment of a moral order which reflected the ethics but not the theology of Calvinism."[42] It would be difficult to overestimate the importance of the Tappan brothers to the cause of reform, especially the abolition of slavery in the United States.

The institution of slavery was a blight on the conscience of

---

[42]Quoted in Mark A. Noll, et. al., *Eerdmans' Handbook to Christianity in America* (Grand Rapids: William B. Eerdmans Publishing Company, 1983), 191.

America from its introduction in Jamestown in 1619. Between 1619 and 1760, approximately half a million Africans were imported as slaves by the thirteen colonies. The invention of the cotton gin in 1793 by Eli Whitney, a Massachusetts inventor, insured the survival of slavery in the southern states long after it ceased to exist in the northern states. The cotton gin made slavery a vital part of the southern economy, dominated by the "Cotton Kingdom" of the Gulf Coast states. Between 1790 and 1860, the slave population grew from seven hundred thousand to 3.5 million. By 1860, one half the dollar value of all American exports was accounted for by southern cotton, much of it destined for the factories in England. So dependent was the southern economy upon slavery that southerners of all classes closed ranks in its defense. Ministers developed elaborate scriptural arguments defending slavery as a positive good for both master and slave. Those who spoke out against it on biblical grounds, as did the Quakers in Virginia, were driven from the South following the Nat Turner insurrection in Southampton County, Virginia, in 1831.

After 1830, the antislavery movement, which had been stronger in the South, shifted to the North. The abolition movement in America, like the other reform movements of the Benevolent Empire, was born in the Second Great Awakening. The leaders of the abolition crusade were men and women converted during the revivals of the 1820s. Theodore Dwight Weld, author of *The Bible Against Slavery* (1837) and *American Slavery As It Is* (1839), was one who took up the cause of abolition following his conversion in 1826 under the preaching of Charles G. Finney.

Weld was a student at Lane Theological Seminary in Cincinnati, Ohio, during the early 1830s. Lane was supported financially by the Tappan brothers and housed a number of students who, like Weld, were converted through Finney's ministry. In 1834, Weld led a series of abolitionist crusades at Lane. When the seminary responded by banning all abolitionist activities, Weld led a mass exodus of most of the students. "The Lane rebels," as they became known, migrated to Lorain County,

Ohio, where they founded Oberlin Collegiate Institute, known as Oberlin College after 1850. Finney joined Oberlin as professor of theology in 1835 and served as president of the college from 1851 to 1866. Under Finney's influence and with financial support from Arthur and Lewis Tappan, Oberlin College became the center of the abolitionist movement prior to the Civil War.

In 1833, the American Anti-Slavery Society was founded. Among those active in it were William Lloyd Garrison, the editor and publisher of the influential abolitionist newspaper, *The Liberator;* John Greenleaf Whittier, a Quaker poet and perhaps the most influential abolitionist writer; Jonathan Blanchard, the first president of Wheaton College (Illinois); and Harriet Beecher Stowe, daughter of Lyman Beecher and author of *Uncle Tom's Cabin, or Life Among the Lowly* (1851–1852). Harriet Beecher Stowe was influenced by her reading of Weld's *Slavery As It Is* to write *Uncle Tom's Cabin,* first serialized in the *National Era.* Her antislavery novel was so influential that President Lincoln is said to have credited her, perhaps half seriously, with starting the Civil War.

Despite the efforts of the Christians among the abolitionists, slavery was not to be ended in America by moral persuasion. It would take the Civil War (1861–1865), the bloodiest war in American history, to cleanse the land of its scourge. Meanwhile, slavery split many denominations during the two decades preceding the Civil War. In 1843, many individuals left the Methodist Episcopal Church to form the Wesleyan Methodist Church with a no-slave-owning membership. In 1845, slave-owning Methodists and Baptists organized the Methodist Episcopal Church, South, and the Southern Baptist Convention. Southern Presbyterians split in 1857 and 1861.

Southern slaves were at first denied access to the gospel. Many slave owners felt the gospel encouraged slave revolts. Indeed, slave insurrections such as Nat Turners' in 1831 were influenced by religion. As time moved on, however, many slave owners became convinced that Christianity could be used to produce more honest and obedient slaves. By the 1840s, many southerners wanted to refute the abolitionist charge that they

AMERICAN CHURCHES SPLIT OVER SLAVERY

Methodists–1844
- Methodist Episcopal Church
- Methodist Episcopal Church, South

Baptists–1845
- American Baptist Missionary Union
- Southern Baptist Convention

- Presbyterian Church in the United States of America
- Presbyterian Church in the Confederate States (after 1865: Presbyterian Church in the United States)

Episcopalians–1861
- Protestant Episcopal Church
- Protestant Episcopal

wanted their slaves to remain heathens. Thus the new southern denominations stepped up efforts to convert the slaves. Many southern church leaders on the eve of the Civil War were proud of their efforts to evangelize the slaves.

But not all was well for free African-Americans in the North before the Civil War. African-Americans were normally restricted to the galleries of churches, where they were expected to worship separate from the white members of the congregation. In 1816, Richard Allen, a former slave who became a Methodist circuit rider, founded the African Methodist Episcopal Church as a union of black churches. By 1856, there were twenty thousand members. In 1821, the African Methodist Episcopal Zion Church was founded, another African-American denomination.

By the middle of the nineteenth century, American evangelicals were losing their zeal for reform. Earlier Christians were united in the belief that they must work towards both spiritual renewal and reform of society. They tended to believe that their efforts would hasten the return of Jesus Christ. Later, however, several developments contributed to the decline in concern for reforming society.

The Benevolent Empire began to break up due to the tension between those who favored moderate and extremist solutions to society's ills. The slave question took its toll as Christians divided into those who favored immediate abolition, those who advocated ultimate abolition, and those who defended slavery. Finally, there was the rise of dispensationalism towards the end of the century.

Dispensationalism, founded by John Nelson Darby, was a response to the growing conviction that Western civilization was degenerating, rather than progressing spiritually—as evangelicals previously believed. It encouraged, as Richard F. Lovelace has pointed out, acceptance of "a form of premillennialism which was evangelistically active but socially passive."[43] More and more evangelicals emphasized spiritual matters, while abandoning or passively supporting their original goal of transforming society.

Another development that tended to wean evangelicals away from social reform was their growing dependence on wealthy entrepreneurs for financial support. Wealthy evangelicals tended to be rugged individualists. They were attracted to a form of Christianity that emphasized evangelism while ignoring or downplaying social responsibility. The Enlightenment view of private property as an inalienable natural right displaced the biblical view of stewardship over God's property. Self-centered individualism was extolled over the virtue of seeing one's self as a responsible member of a community. The quest for a more just order of society was left to the theologically liberal advocates of the social gospel.

The social gospel represented a shift in emphasis from the salvation of the individual to the reform of society's institutions. It was perhaps an overreaction to the shift among evangelicals toward an emphasis on evangelism to the exclusion of institutional reform. Just as evangelicals were embracing a form of premillennialism that saw the institutional church and Christian civilization in decline, the advocates of the social gospel

[43]*Dynamics of Spiritual Life*, 377.

believed that the kingdom of God on earth could be realized through economic and political reform.

The two most important figures among the social gospelers were Washington Gladden and Walter Rauschenbusch. Gladden, a Congregationalist minister from Columbus, Ohio, believed that the rugged *laissez-faire* economics of the day perpetuated the injustices in society. Gladden felt that by not addressing the problem, the mainline churches were becoming irrelevant to the working class. To address these injustices, Gladden advocated the right of labor to unionize, encouraged profit-sharing programs, and called for arbitration of industrial disputes. He also attempted to persuade his denomination to refuse a large contribution from Standard Oil.

Walter Rauschenbusch, considered the "Father of the Social Gospel in America," was pastor of the Second German Baptist Church in New York City, where he witnessed firsthand the exploitation of the laboring classes—especially the newly arrived immigrants. In a series of books published between 1910 and 1917, Rauschenbusch called for a rethinking of Christian theology that would make God and the gospel relevant to the modern world. The kingdom of God rightly understood was "a social system working for the equality of all people."[44]

The social gospel of Gladden and Rauschenbusch reached the general public through the phenomenally popular novel, *In His Steps* (1896). Charles M. Sheldon, a Congregationalist pastor from Kansas, simply asked what might happen in a small town where everyone modeled their lives after the example of Jesus Christ. The novel has sold more than 23 million copies since its first appearance, according to some estimates, and remains a popular novel among Christian readers.

FOREIGN MISSIONS
. . . .

Evangelicals may have abdicated one important area of the gospel to theologically liberal social gospelers, but in the area of foreign

[44]George M. Marsden, *Religion and American Culture* (New York: Harcourt Brace Jovanovich, Publishers, 1990), 120.

missions, they continued to forge ahead throughout the whole nineteenth century. The nineteenth century was the great century of Protestant missions. Protestants showed remarkably little interest in taking the gospel beyond Europe (except to the North American colonies) during the first two hundred years after the Reformation. What interest there was prior to the nineteenth century came from the German Pietists in the eighteenth century. King Frederick IV of Denmark and Norway sought help from the Pietist leader August Hermann Francke in recruiting missionaries to serve in his foreign possessions, especially southern India. Among those who heeded the call were Bartholomew Ziegenbalg and Christian Friedrich Schwartz. The most remarkable Protestant foreign mission effort prior to the nineteenth century, however, was that of the Moravian Brethren under the leadership of Count Nicholaus Ludwig von Zinzendorf (see chapter 7).

The birth of modern Protestant foreign missions is often associated with the work of William Carey (1761–1834), although that honor is more appropriately given to Count Zinzendorf. Carey was a tent-making (i.e., supporting himself by his own income, rather than receiving support as a minister) Baptist preacher from England, who became a missionary in India in 1793. In 1792, he published *An Enquiry into the Obligation of Christians to Use Means for the Conversion of the Heathens,* in which he reminded Christians of the Lord's command to "preach the gospel to every creature." The Baptist Missionary Society was founded in 1793 as a direct result of Carey's efforts. In India, Carey translated the New Testament into Bengali, published grammars and dictionaries, and translated Eastern books. He was instrumental in founding mission schools and promoting agricultural improvements. All in all, Carey's efforts resulted in six complete Bible translations and another twenty-four partial translations. William Carey set a standard and an example that inspired numerous missionaries during the nineteenth century.

Interest in foreign missions among Protestants in the United States began with a group of students converted during the Second Great Awakening. Among them was Adoniram Judson. At

Andover Theological Seminary, Judson met a small group of students who had committed their lives to foreign missions. In 1810, the group was able to get the Congregational church to found the American Board of Commissioners for Foreign Missions. Two years later, Adoniram Judson and his wife of only thirteen days set out for India with six others appointed by the American Board. They were the first foreign missionaries from America.

During the voyage to India, the group engaged in a Bible study together, the end result of which was their conviction that infant baptism and sprinkling were both unscriptural. The Judsons and Luther Rice, another of the six missionaries, decided to leave the Congregational church and join the American Baptists. As a result, the General Missionary Convention of the Baptist Denomination in the United States of America for Foreign Missions was founded in 1814. The Judsons went on to serve as career missionaries in Burma. Their story, which includes imprisonment, deep depression, and martyrdom, as well as triumphs, is one of the truly great inspirational stories in the history of foreign missionary work.

The Judsons were supported by a foreign mission board, as was William Carey and most of those who went out to the mission field in the nineteenth century. Others tried supporting themselves, as did Karl Gutzloff, who labored alone in China during the 1830s and 1840s. James Hudson Taylor went to China in 1853 with support from the Chinese Evangelization Society. In 1857, Taylor resigned from the Society and tried to continue on his own until ill health forced him to return to England in 1860. In 1865, he founded the China Inland Mission, the first interdenominational faith mission.

Taylor took George Müller (1805–1898) as his example. Müller, a member of the Plymouth Brethren, founded an orphanage in Bristol, England. Müller never made a public appeal for financial support, but trusted God to supply the orphanage's needs. Taylor resolved to do likewise with the China Inland Mission. He asked only for prayer support and specific numbers of missionaries, but never financial support.[45] Other innovations introduced by Hudson Taylor, such as accepting candidates without formal training, requiring missionaries to adopt native dress, and locating control on the field, became common practice among foreign missions in the second half of the century.

The relationship between foreign missionaries and Western imperialism was always a difficult one. Doors that would have otherwise remained closed to missionaries were opened by Western military might. After its defeat in the second Opium War, China, for example, was forced by the Treaty of Tientsin (1858) to open its territory to both opium and missionaries. Missionaries often enjoyed the protection of Western arms but could also be caught in the middle of colonial wars, as was the case with the Judsons.

Like the Jesuits who tried to protect the Latin American Indians from exploitation by European colonialists during the sixteenth and seventeenth centuries, the nineteenth-century missionaries tried to mitigate the evils of imperialism. They were often critical of government policies in the colonies and the economic exploitation by Western settlers. British evangelicals believed that the English owed a debt to Africans because of the slave trade and to India because of the vast amounts of wealth they took. This is not to say that missionaries opposed colonial rule, however. Western rule of the non-European world was taken for granted throughout the nineteenth century by Christians and non-Christians alike. Christians tended to justify it in their own minds by interpreting the "Westernization" of the world as the same as the "Christianization" of the world. The advance of Christian civilization in the world would, many Christians believed, hasten the return of Jesus Christ.

No religious justification can be given for imperialism, however. Christians cannot justify the political domination of one people by another. Still, to be fair, one must recognize the successes made by missionaries in bringing light to areas of the

[45] Among the more than forty "faith" missions that were influenced by Taylor's "faith principle" were the Christian and Missionary Alliance (1887), The Evangelical Alliance Mission (1890), the Central American Mission (1890), the Sudan Interior Mission (1893), and the Africa Inland Mission (1895).

world where people had been enslaved for centuries by the forces of darkness. Wherever the missionaries went with the gospel, they brought Western values rooted in Christianity. The value and dignity of the individual—especially women—was virtually unknown outside the Western world. Missionaries fought against the slave trade in Africa; the practice of burning alive widows with their deceased husbands (*sati*) and the caste system in India; the cruel practices of foot binding in China; and female genital mutilation in Africa.[46] Often they met strong opposition from white settlers, who saw the missionaries' struggle for justice as a threat to their economic interests.

If missionaries willingly, or unwillingly, aided the rise of imperialism in the nineteenth century, they also contributed to its eventual demise. The nationalists who would later lead the movement for independence from European rule were often educated in mission schools and based their arguments on Christian teachings. Also, missionaries often sympathized openly with the aspirations of the nationalist leaders. Such support for justice brought them into conflict with the European settlers, who saw the missionaries as a threat to their ongoing livelihood. John Philip, for example, labored tirelessly for an end to forced labor and for recognition of the civil rights of all people of color in England's Cape Town colony.

To tell the story of nineteenth-century missions and mention only the names of the great male missionaries is to tell only half the story. Foreign missions was one area of church life in the nineteenth century where women, although not ordained, "could preach, evangelize, plant churches, educate national leaders, and carry on humanitarian work."[47] Ann Hasseltine Judson and Jennie Faulding Taylor labored alongside their husbands as equal partners, sharing the triumphs and tragedies of the mission field.

Not all women on the mission field were wives of missionar-

---

[46]Many of these "relics of barbarism," as they were called by turn-of-the-century Europeans, have made strong comebacks since the end of colonialism after World War II. The cruel practice of female genital mutilation has even made inroads in American society, where an estimated forty thousand girls as young as four are permanently physically and emotionally harmed by the procedure (*The New York Times*, 8 August 1996).

[47]Robert G. Clouse, et. al., *Two Kingdoms*, 506.

ies. Many went as single missionaries, achieving fame rivaling
that of any man. Charlotte (Lottie) Diggs Moon, the "Patron
Saint of Southern Baptist Missions," labored successfully in
northern China where other missionaries had failed. She is
remembered in an annual Christmas missions offering collected
in Southern Baptist churches. Dr. Ida Sophia Scudder opened a
hospital, nursing school, and medical college for women in
India. Amy Carmichael went to India in 1895, where she
founded Dohnavur Fellowship as a home for abused youth, especially girls who were rescued from a life of temple prostitution.
She also founded the Sisters of the Common Life, a Protestant
religious order that provided a family for single women. It was
patterned after the Brethren of the Common Life, founded by
Geert Groote (see chapter 5). And then there was Mary Slessor,
who was inspired by the death of David Livingston to volunteer
for mission work along the Calabar coast of West Africa.

Mary Slessor believed that single women represented less of a
threat to the unreached tribes than did men. Therefore, she set out
to pioneer missions among the Okoyong people, where white men
had previously failed. Slessor identified with the Okoyong to the
extent of living in mud huts "infested with roaches, rats, and
ants,"[48] and abandoning European dress for the more cli-
mate-appropriate native garments. Paying little attention to health
and hygiene, Mary Slessor "lived native," as other missionaries
said of her. She spent almost forty years in West Africa, thirty-six
in a mud hut, and died at age sixty-three, lovingly remembered by
those whom she served as the "Mother of All the Peoples."

THE CHALLENGE OF HIGHER CRITICISM AND LIBERALISM

The great revivals, the struggle against slavery and for reform of
society's institutions, and the tremendous advance in foreign missions is not the whole story of the church in the nineteenth century.
It was during the nineteenth century that Satan counterattacked, and

[48]Ruth A. Tucker, *From Jerusalem to Irian Jaya: A Biographical History of Christian Missions* (Grand Rapids: Academic Books, 1983),162.

did so with astonishing success. It was a new version of the old lie, "Hath God really said?" aimed at undermining people's faith in the inspiration and integrity of the Bible. The rise of higher criticism of the Bible and theological liberalism would eventually lead to the conviction among many that the Bible was only a human book, a human attempt to understand what was ultimately unknowable. For many, God would become silent, and humanity would be left alone without any absolutes to give guidance in matters of either faith or practice. The slide that began with the Enlightenment continued in the nineteenth century.

If the Enlightenment led to unbelief based on skepticism, by the end of the nineteenth century, unbelief appeared to be based on a firm foundation of "fact." This shift was due in no small part to the influence of two individuals, the German philosopher Georg W. F. Hegel and the English biologist Charles Darwin. Both appeared to provide convincing evidence for the nonhistoricity of Scripture. Since, to many, the truth of Christianity rests on the Bible providing truth with regard to the historical events described in it, the theories of Hegel and Darwin presented a serious challenge.

Hegel published his ideas during the first decade of the nineteenth century. In his view, the universe, humanity's understanding of it, and truth itself, are all continually unfolding. This evolutionary process will continue without end. Thus, there is no possibility of anything absolute. In the area of truth, this means that what is considered truth today is but an evolutionary synthesis of all past truths. Likewise, what is considered truth today will be contained in tomorrow's synthesis. All truth is, therefore, relative.

The implications of Hegel's philosophy for how people should view the Bible were profound. If there is no absolute truth, then the Bible cannot be absolutely true. The Bible is only a product of a historical process. What it says is only what its authors believed God to be saying in their day and cannot be regarded as authoritative for people living in the modern age. Just as the Bible was not the final word on how humans have viewed God, likewise, Christ was not the final revelation, nor the Cross the final word on the Atonement.

Hegel was only expressing the consensus of the educated people of his day. The same may be said of the theories of Charles Darwin. Evolutionary theories can be found among the ancient Greek philosophers. Darwin's *On the Origin of Species* (1859) and *The Descent of Man* (1871) appeared at just the right time in the history of Western civilization. The ideas they contained received enthusiastic reception and by the 1890s were accepted as fact, even though learned scholars demonstrated that no scientific observation or experiment could be offered to support them.

More than anything else, Darwin's theory of biological evolution contributed to the demise of traditional religion and the rise of a secular spirit. Virtually every thinking person accepted the claim that Darwin had provided scientific evidence that human beings evolved from lower forms of animal life. The historicity of the Bible was destroyed for many. Reason, supported by the truth claims of science, became the final authority—not the Bible. What was left was a world without design populated by people without souls. In 1882, Friedrich Nietzsche (1844–1900), an early German existentialist philosopher, announced the death of God in *The Joyful Wisdom.* Though few were so bold, many implicitly agreed with him.

Theological liberalism arose as an attempt to salvage Christianity as a value-creating movement from its seeming total destruction by the Enlightenment and the alleged discoveries of nineteenth-century science. It appeared first in the German universities and then spread throughout Europe, Great Britain, and the United States. Chief among its exponents were Friedrich Schleiermacher and Albrecht Ritschl in Europe, and Harry Emerson Fosdick in the United States. The big shift to liberalism in the United States came in 1880. By 1890, every major American denomination was moving rapidly toward liberalism.

The liberals embraced the higher-critical view of the Bible, by which the individual critic searched for the hidden meaning behind the biblical text. Darwinian evolution was assumed and creation rejected. Miracles were dismissed as impossible. God became a universal spirit, Christ only a "God-filled" man, and redemption only a kind of "God-consciousness," which meant being in tune with the universal spirit. Sin was dismissed as myth, while salvation became universal. No one has provided a better description of liberalism than H. Richard Niebuhr, who observed that in liberalism, "A God without wrath brought men without sin into a kingdom without judgment through the ministration of a Christ without a cross."[49]

Having rejected the Bible as the final authority, the liberals sought to ground their faith in religious experience. Schleiermacher taught that an individual's religion was not found in doctrines, creeds, or confessions, but in "a deep psychological experience of dependence upon some indefinable Reality." God could be felt, but not really known. The basic question became, "How do I explain my experience?" not, "How does Scripture explain my experience?" The basis of authority had shifted from the Bible to personal religious experience.

Like the great humanists of the Enlightenment, the liberals were very optimistic. Basic to their theology was an unbounded confidence in human reason and a fundamentally evolutionary worldview. Here we can see the marriage of Hegel and Darwin. Humans are progressing (evolving) both spiritually and biologically. Progress is not only individual, but also collective, for society is also progressing. Ultimately, all of humanity will be "redeemed" in some future utopia. This optimism was reinforced by events within secular history. The industrial revolution and European imperialism tended to support the liberal's faith in the perfectibility (redemption) of humanity. Classical liberalism exhibited a vulnerability to reality, however. To maintain that sin was simply a lack of God-consciousness would become increasingly more difficult in the twentieth century. Two world wars, the Holocaust, and the Soviet labor camps would disillusion many liberals by the mid-twentieth century, requiring them to reinvent theological liberalism by embracing neo-orthodoxy.

[49] Quoted in *Eerdmans' Handbook to the History of Christianity,* 598.

TIMELINE FOR CHAPTER 9

1793	William Carey leaves for missionary work in India
	Baptist Missionary Society founded
1793	Eli Whitney's cotton gin is invented
1807	Slavery is abolished in British West Indies
1812	Adoniram Judson leaves for missionary work in Burma
1816	African Methodist Episcopal Church founded
1823	British and Foreign Anti-Slavery Society founded
1826	American Temperance Society founded
1831	Nat Turner's insurrection in Virginia
1833	Parliament abolishes slavery in the British Empire
	Parliament passes Factory Act of 1833
1842	Parliament passes Mines Act of 1842
1845–1861	American churches split over slavery issue
1851–1852	Harriet Beecher Stowe publishes *Uncle Tom's Cabin*
1851–1866	Charles G. Finney serves as president of Oberlin College
1858	Treaty of Tientsin opens up China to missionaries
1859	Charles Darwin's *On the Origin of Species* (biological evolution)
1861–1865	American Civil War
1865	Hudson Taylor founds China Inland Mission
1871	Charles Darwin's *The Descent of Man*
1875	Parliament passes Climbing Boys Act
1876	Mary Slessor leaves for missionary work in West Africa
1895	Amy Carmichael leaves for missionary work in India
1896	Chars M. Sheldon publishes *In His Steps*

CHAPTER TEN

Age of Anxiety: The Church in the Twentieth Century

THE BIG PICTURE

During the twentieth century, Christianity faced its greatest challenge since the birth of the church at Pentecost. In response to two world wars, the Great Depression, the Holocaust of European Jewry, and the threat of nuclear and/or environmental annihilation, people sought new answers to the most basic questions of ultimate meaning. The result was a paradigm shift in worldview. Meaning was abandoned as those outside Christianity embraced a world void of meaning. Anxiety and despair characterized the lives of many in the twentieth century. For the church, the shift meant the passing of liberalism (or modernism), and then neo-orthodoxy, as non-evangelicals opted for even more radical theologies that reflected the assumptions of secular philosophies at the end of the century. Evangelicals diversified. There were not only fundamentalists and mainstream evangelicals, but also neo-evangelicals, charismatics, and Pentecostals, among others. Believers in the historic faith within the Roman Catholic church embraced similar beliefs. By the end of the century and the dawn of a new millennium, the church in the non-Western world experienced impressive growth, while Europe and North America became mission fields for a variety of non-Christian religious worldviews.

KEY EVENTS

1909	Publication of the *Scofield Reference Bible* popularizes premillenialism and dispensationalism.
1925	The Scopes "Monkey" Trial in Dayton, Tennessee, symbolizes the defeat of fundamentalism as an agent for shaping American culture.
1949	Billy Graham's Los Angeles tent revival launches a new era of mass evangelism worldwide.
1962–1965	With the Vatican II Council, the Roman Catholic church begins to respond to the postmodern world, while also welcoming a dialogue with Protestants.
1974	With the Lausanne Congress on World Evangelism, evangelicals begin to respond to the postmodern world with evangelism and social action.

What was perhaps the single most important event in the twentieth century occurred at 11:15 on Sunday morning, June 28, 1914. Gavrilo Princip, a nineteen-year-old Serbian nationalist, shot and killed Francis Ferdinand, Archduke and heir to the throne of Austria-Hungary, and his wife Sophie Chotek in the Bosnian town of Sarajevo. The crisis that followed led to the outbreak of World War I in August 1914. World War I was the most traumatic event in the history of Western civilization since the fall of the Roman Empire. The twentieth century is often called the "Age of Anxiety," because it left the future of Western civilization in doubt. But World War I did not cause the Age of Anxiety; it only acted as a catalyst for trends that were established before 1914.

During the decades before World War I, a second scientific revolution and a new set of intellectuals brought forth theories and scientific discoveries that called into question the individual's relationship to the universe. Were humans reasoning, rational beings in an orderly, meaningful universe, or irrational animals adrift in a universe of chaos? For many thinking individuals, the experience of World War I, followed by the Great Depression, the Second World War, the Holocaust, and the Cold War, made the need for answers to the most basic questions of ultimate meaning even more urgent. The disintegration of the Enlightenment tradition accelerated, as did the drift towards a new understanding of reality—often referred to as postmodernism.

The disintegration of the Enlightenment tradition, or modernism, made the twentieth century an era of shifting ideologies. The implications for the history of Christianity during the century were profound. Theological liberalism, based as it was on the Enlightenment, peaked and then broke down after World War I, giving way to the rise of neo-orthodoxy. Neo-orthodoxy was better suited to the uncertainties of the 1920s through the 1960s. As postmodernism gained ground in the general culture, neo-orthodoxy yielded the field to more radical theologies during the 1960s, 1970s, and 1980s.

Those denominations that embraced theologies that abandoned biblical authority suffered a decline in both membership and influence. Efforts to stem the tide of decline, such as ecumenism and social action, had little effect other than to widen the gap between these denominations and those that reaffirmed their commitment to the historic teachings of the church as defined by the great church councils and the Reformation.

Those who identified with the historic faith took on new life during the twentieth century. These "evangelical" churches tended to increase their membership, while the liberal churches declined. During the century, evangelicalism demonstrated a remarkable ability to diversify while holding to the fundamentals of the historic faith. This was especially true during the second half of the century. One began to speak of "mainstream" evangelicalism as well as a "neo-evangelicalism." The Jesus People, various Pentecostal, charismatic, and even "Third Wave" groups appeared under the evangelical umbrella. Parachurch organizations, too, proliferated, as evangelicals cooperated outside denominations to spread the gospel to "non-churched" people groups.

The Roman Catholic church abandoned its self-imposed exile to engage the modern world and attempted to assume once again the moral leadership of Christendom. Pope John XXIII's brief reign (1958–1963) opened the windows of the Roman Catholic church to the modern world. John XXIII called a new ecumenical council, Vatican II, with the goal of bringing the church up to date. The laity were addressed as the "people of God," and Protestants, now called "separated brethren," were welcomed in dialogue with Roman Catholics. The century ended with the papal throne occupied by John-Paul II (1978-), the "millennial pope," perhaps the most popular pope in the church's history, despite his very conservative positions on key doctrinal issues. Given the examples of John-Paul II and Mother Teresa, the saint of Calcutta, it was little wonder that Protestant evangelicals at the end of the century began to speak of cooperation between Roman Catholics and Protestants—despite the doctrinal differences that sparked the Reformation four hundred years earlier.

During the last quarter of the century, the believing church experienced its most impressive growth in the developing nations of the Third World. In 1914, Christians were still a very small minority outside the West. By the end of the century, the world's largest churches, sometimes called "mega" or even "superchurches," were located outside traditional Christendom. While the birthplace of the church in the Middle East remained under Islam and the lands of the Reformation slipped rapidly into a post-Christian, postmodern, secular culture, revival swept through Africa, Asia, and Latin America. There were, for example, only eighty thousand Roman Catholics and ninety-six thousand Protestants in Korea in 1914. By the mid-1990s, Seoul alone had more than sixteen hundred churches, including Yoido Full Gospel Church with its eight hundred thousand members and fifty-five thousand deacons.

DEFENDING THE FAITH: AMERICA

World War I brought to the forefront the fact that America was no longer a homogeneous nation and the bulwark of Protestant Christianity. The war in Europe, and America's participation in it, presented a serious challenge to churches in America. Both liberals and conservatives, Protestants and Roman Catholics, responded to the war with enthusiasm. For all but the historic pacifist churches

(Quakers and Mennonites), the war was a crusade to save Christian civilization in general and preserve a Christian America.

Evangelical Christians were quick to view the United States as God's agent in a holy war against the evil personified in Germany. It became increasingly difficult to distinguish patriotism from Christianity, as American civil religion pushed the latter into the background. "Christianity and patriotism are synonymous terms," said evangelist Billy Sunday (1862–1935), "and hell and traitors are synonymous."[50]

President Woodrow Wilson's references to the war as "the war to end all wars" and the war to "make the world safe for democracy" had special meaning for liberal Christians. In tune with the Enlightenment tradition, the liberals had faith in the perfectibility of humanity. They believed that the world was making steady progress towards a future utopia on earth. For them, the progress of democratic Western civilization was the steady advance of Christianity in the world. The war, however, and the failed peace that followed, appeared to confirm what many suspected—that the liberals were wrong about human nature being innately good. Although the impact of the war delivered a death-blow to theological liberalism in Europe, it was the Great Depression that did likewise in the United States. Meanwhile, evangelicals and liberals engaged in a struggle for control of the churches in America during the 1920s.

During the 1920s, many Americans felt that the Christian foundations of American society were under attack and in danger of faltering. The passage of the Eighteenth Amendment to the Constitution in 1919, banning the sale of alcoholic beverages, was a hollow victory. The triumph of communism in Russia in 1917 led to a "Red Scare" in the United States in 1919. Culture was secularized and morals relaxed during the 1920s, the age of jazz and the flapper. Sex, taboo as a subject of polite conversation before World War I, was openly discussed after the war as women became increasingly liberated and Sigmund Freud

---

[50]Quoted in Mark A. Noll, et. al., *Eerdmans' Handbook to Christianity in America* (Grand Rapids, MI: William B. Eerdmans Publishing Co., 1983), 369.

became a popular icon. Sensing that the battle to defend Christian morality was being lost, conservatives reacted with passage of the Johnson-Reed Act (1924) to limit foreign immigration and the infiltration of foreign ideas.

The 1920s were dominated by the so-called fundamentalist-modernist controversy. The battle lines were drawn up before World War I. Bible scholars like A. A. Hodge, Benjamin B. Warfield, Francis L. Patton, and A. T. Robertson defended the "plenary and verbal inspiration and inerrancy" of the Bible in the "original autographs." This emphasis on biblical inerrancy was combined with premillenialism and dispensationalism as popularized by J. N. Darby, William E. Blackstone, and especially C. I. Scofield in the *Scofield Reference Bible* (1909). Bible colleges such as Nyack Missionary College (1882), Moody Bible Institute (1886), Toronto Bible Institute (1884), Bible Institute of Los Angeles (1908), and Prairie Bible Institute (1922) were founded to produce "gap men," who would stand in the gap between the people in the pews and the growing number of liberal pastors coming out of liberal seminaries. Between 1910 and 1915 the twelve-volume work, *The Fundamentals*, was published with contributions from Warfield, Scofield, and many other conservatives.

The chief spokesperson for evangelicals was J. Gresham Machen of Princeton Theological Seminary. In his classic, *Christianity and Liberalism* (1923), Machen argued that liberal Christianity was not Christian at all, but rather "a new religion of humanity and progress" opposed to biblical Christianity. Machen called upon liberals to leave the Christian churches, but it was the evangelicals who more often left to found new denominations. In 1935, Machen was brought before a church court, found guilty of insubordination, and expelled from the Presbyterian Church in the USA.

For many Americans the event that most symbolized the growing irrelevance of conservative Christianity to modern culture was the famous Scopes Trial in Dayton, Tennessee, in July 1925. It was the first trial broadcast across America by radio. The atmosphere in Dayton was like that of a carnival. H. L.

Mencken, the most popular American journalist of the time, described the crowd in Dayton as "peasants and ignoramuses." It was an image that has ever since accompanied the terms "fundamentalist" and "fundamentalism."

William Jennings Bryan (1860–1925), the three-time presidential candidate and one of the greatest Christian statesmen in American history, accepted an invitation to serve as a prosecuting attorney for the trial. Bryan understood that the logic of Darwin's theory of evolution is that there is no right or wrong regarding behavior. Whatever is, is right. Love as a motivating force is replaced by the ethic of struggle, the law of the jungle. Here was the philosophical justification for the new age of materialism. If Darwinism is true, then no one can say that the exploitation of the weak by the strong is wrong. In the jungle, "justice" and "injustice" are meaningless words.

In the course of the trial, Bryan agreed to take the stand as an expert witness on the Bible—which he was not. Bryan was an educated layman who had written many books and articles on biblical subjects, but he was neither a theologian nor a scientist. He certainly was no match for the clever defense attorney (and agnostic), Clarence Darrow. Darrow humiliated Bryan on the witness stand by making him (and by implication those Christians who were opposed to the theory of biological evolution) appear to be ignorant fundamentalists defending the indefensible.

Bryan had in his briefcase a twenty-six page summation, which contained his fears concerning evolution and what its acceptance would really mean. But it remained in his briefcase. The trial was sent to the jury without final arguments. Shortly after the trial, Bryan died in his sleep on July 26, 1925. The popular image of Bryan and fundamentalist Christianity at the famous monkey trial (especially as sensationalized and distorted in the film, *Inherit the Wind* [1960]), is the one that has survived. It is the image of agrarian ingnorance fighting a losing battle to prevent progress and enlightenment.

DEFENDING THE FAITH: EUROPE
. . . .

The struggle for truth in Europe took a somewhat different form from that in America. In the United States, the existence of the churches as legal institutions was never questioned. There, the struggle was one of truth versus falsehood. In Europe during the 1930s and 1940s, the struggle was not only for truth, but the continued existence of the church as a visible institution. The rise of totalitarianism, a new form of authoritarian rule particular to the twentieth century, brought perhaps the most serious challenge to Christianity in modern history.

Totalitarianism, whether of the right (Nazism, Fascism) or the left (Marxism-Leninism, communism), is a surrogate religion based in atheistic materialism. Like any religion, it seeks to answer the perennial questions about ultimate meaning and the purpose of life. Its goal is to produce a "born again" believer in the ideology as embodied in the state. Therefore, it cannot tolerate any ideology or individual with an absolute standard by which to judge the actions of the state or the truth claims of the official ideology. For that reason, totalitarianism must always, eventually, persecute Christianity. Tragically, conservative Christians have often mistakenly seen in right-wing totalitarianism an ally against leftist totalitarianism (communism). They have either actively or passively assisted its rise to power, only to discover too late that the supposed ally was in fact an alternative religious faith that would tolerate no rival for the individual's allegiance.

Karl Marx taught that all religion was like a drug given to the oppressed masses to numb their senses or like a garland of flowers that hides from sight the chains that bind them. To liberate the masses, to achieve their freedom from oppression, religion must be destroyed. The flowers must be plucked away so that the enslaved can see the chains that bind them. Only then will they rise up and proclaim their freedom.

Thus, when Marx's followers came to power in Russia in 1917, they immediately launched an attack upon the churches.

Freedom of religion and the freedom of antireligious propaganda became a constitutional right. Viewing Christianity as an obstacle to progress and a rival worldview, they closed the churches, seized their property, and forbade them to continue their traditional charitable and educational work. Christians were forbidden to meet for worship or other purposes without government permission. The persecution became particularly severe after Joseph Stalin, a former seminary student, came to power in 1924. Only during World War II, when the survival of the Soviet Union was in doubt, was the persecution of Christians eased in an effort to rally the Russian people in a Great Patriotic War to defend Mother Russia.

Pope Pius XI (1903–1939) expressed the opinion of most Christians, when in 1937 he declared in *Divini Redemptoris* that "communism is intrinsically wrong and no one who would save Christian civilization may collaborate with it in any undertaking whatsoever."[51] Unfortunately, many Christians—both Catholic and Protestant—mistakenly saw in the rise of right-wing totalitarianism in Germany a bulwark against the spread of atheistic communism.

Unlike communism, National Socialism, or Nazism for short, did not openly proclaim an atheistic ideology. In fact, Adolf Hitler was very vocal in his denunciation of communism.[52] What many did not see, or chose not to see, was that Hitler understood both communism and Christianity to be evil inventions of the Jews, that "culture-destroying race." "The heaviest blow that ever struck humanity," declared Hitler, "was the coming of Christianity. Bolshevism is Christianity's illegitimate child. Both are inventions of the Jew."[53]

The anti-Semitic note in Hitler's attack on communism did not alert many Christians to the hidden dangers of Nazi ideology. Anti-Semitism was all too common among Christians during the

---

[51] Quoted in Robert G. Clouse, et. al., *Two Kingdoms,* 560.
[52] Hitler was raised a Roman Catholic and even served as a choirboy in the local Catholic church. When he died on April 30, 1945, Masses were said for him in Catholic churches, until it was learned that he had committed suicide.
[53] Quoted in Robert G. Clouse, et. al., *Two Kingdoms,* 555.

interwar years. In America, fundamentalists rallied against President Franklin D. Roosevelt's "Jewish New Deal," as a plot by leftist radicals to destroy capitalism and traditional American values. By opposing efforts to relieve the suffering caused by the Great Depression and by opposing passage of the Twenty-first Amendment to repeal prohibition, fundamentalists in America lost all potential for helping to shape American society for generations to come. They left the battlefield to retreat into denominational ghettos.

Hitler's call for a "positive Christianity" and his pro-moral, pro-family policies lulled many Christians into a false sense of security. On July 20, 1933, the Vatican signed the *Reichkonkordat* with the new Nazi government of Germany. In exchange for a guarantee of its right to exist as an institution and operate Christian schools, the Catholic church recognized the legitimacy of the Nazi government and withdrew from all political activity. Thereafter, any Catholic citizen who chose to oppose Nazi policies had to do so as a private citizen. Later, when the Nazis violated the terms of the concordat, the church did protest. When the evil nature of Nazi racial ideology became apparent, individual Catholic leaders did publicly denounce such policies. On August 3, 1941, Clemens von Galen, Bishop of Munster, denounced the Nazi euthanasia program as evil. There was such a public outcry that Hitler saw political wisdom in temporarily halting the euthanasia program. In 1937, the same year that Pius IX issued the encyclical *Divini Redemptoris* against communism, he also issued *Mit brennender Sorge* ("With burning sorrow"), sharply condemning Nazi folk ideology as heresy.

Protestants in Germany gave a mixed response to the rise of Nazism. As early as 1932, a "German Christian" movement—conservative, nationalistic, and anti-Semitic—was organized. Proclaiming themselves the "SA of Jesus Christ," they adopted the slogan, "The swastika on our breast, the Cross in our heart." Many young pastors and theological students joined the Nazi party. On September 27, 1933, Ludwig Muller, an army chaplain, was elected Reich Bishop by the National Synod of the

German Evangelical Church Confederation, which was held in Wittenberg. Between 1933 and 1937, a relentless persecution of the smaller Protestant denominations was pursued. The pacifist churches were effectively destroyed in 1938, when draft resistance became a capital offense.

At the National Synod of 1937 that elected Ludwig Muller as Reich Bishop, Martin Niemoeller, a former U-boat commander and pastor from Berlin-Dahlem, denounced the "German Christian" movement. Niemoeller called for a return to a free, evangelical church. When, in November 1933, the followers of Ludwig Muller called for abolishing the Old Testament and the "Jewish" theology of the apostle Paul from the New Testament, while proclaiming Jesus Christ to have been an "Aryan," half of Germany's Protestant pastors rallied to Niemoeller's cause.

At Barmen, in May 1934, the Confessing Church (*Bekennende Kirche*) was organized by Niemoeller and his supporters in opposition to the "German Christians." The Barmen Declaration, drafted by theologian Karl Barth (1886–1968), declared the Confessing Church's commitment to the authority of Scripture and called upon the "German Christians" to return to the historic Christian faith.

The Confessing Church was repudiated or ignored by most Protestant leaders. Its leaders were harassed and imprisoned by the Gestapo. After proclaiming in a sermon on June 27, 1937, that Christians must not remain silent but speak out as God commands, Niemoeller was arrested and imprisoned in concentration camps until 1945. When Karl Barth was ordered to begin his lectures at the University of Bonn with the fascist "Heil Hitler!" salute, he left Germany. Dietrich Bonhoeffer (1906–1945), who served as director of the Confessing Church's illegal seminary on the Baltic Sea, became involved in the German resistance movement. After being implicated in a plot to assassinate Hitler (July 20, 1944), Bonhoeffer was arrested and imprisoned. He was executed on April 9, 1945, by special order of Hitler.

THE RISE AND DEMISE OF NEO-ORTHODOXY

Just as liberalism arose as an attempt to salvage Christianity from total destruction by the Enlightenment and nineteenth-century science, neo-orthodoxy was an attempt to salvage liberalism from the realities of twentieth-century history. The event that is usually taken as marking the demise of liberalism and the appearance of neo-orthodoxy (or existential theology) is the publication of Karl Barth's *Commentary on Romans* in 1919. It infiltrated American seminaries and churches after the Great Depression and delivered the deathblow to classical liberalism in America. By the mid-1930s even leading liberals like Harry Emerson Fosdick were admitting that liberalism was no longer tenable.

Many of Barth's followers accepted the higher-critical view of Scripture. They held that the Bible is a human book, and an erring human witness to revelation. It is not divinely revealed, propositional, objective truth. The truth of Scripture is not found in the accuracy of the written record—it is an existential truth, which has the capacity to transform lives.

According to neo-orthodox views, the writers of Scripture were attempting to record in human words their religious experiences. In their experiences, they encountered God. But God's truth cannot be contained in human words, because revelation is a matter of nonverbal living experience. The biblical writers recorded their experiences as best they could, given their limited understanding of science, and so forth. The more sophisticated, twentieth-century readers of Scripture, therefore, must interpret what they read subjectively. They cannot know for sure what actually happened when the gospel writers claimed to have come face-to-face with the physically risen Christ, nor what actually happened to Paul on the road to Damascus. By reading the accounts with faith, however, readers today can also hope to have a religious experience that will transform and give meaning to their life.

Because of their basic belief that God is so "wholly other" that human words cannot accurately convey his revelation, those who adhere to neo-orthodoxy are forced to ground authority in the subjective experience of the individual. Each individual is his own authority, relying on his experience. It is, therefore, impossible to know if anyone has ever apprehended—or will ever apprehend—the truth. There is no possibility for absolutes in doctrine or in morality.

Among the followers of Barth and neo-orthodoxy were Emil Brunner (1886–1965), Reinhold Niebuhr (1893–1971), Paul Tillich (1886–1965), John Robinson (1919–1983), and Rudolf Bultmann (1884–1976). Bultmann, and especially Tillich, went well beyond Barth. For Tillich, who emigrated to the United States from Germany in 1933, religion was "ultimate concern," God was the monotheistic "ground of being," and sin was only estrangement from that "ground of being." With Tillich and Bultmann, neo-orthodoxy began to lose relevance during the 1960s. More radical theologies vied with one another for the ears of willing listeners. The theology of hope, process theology, and liberation theologies all sought salvation in history through human effort.

POST-WORLD WAR II

When World War II ended, the world was spiritually very different from what it was at the opening of the century. Europe, the home of the Reformation and the great evangelical and pietist revivals, was now a spiritual wasteland. Enlightenment thought and liberal theology, combined with the reality of the Holocaust, had taken its toll spiritually. Neo-orthodoxy was not the balm needed for Western civilization's troubled conscience. At the end of the twentieth century, Europe was a mission field—not only for missionaries carrying the gospel of biblical Christianity, but also for a great host of religious teachers and gurus from the non-Christian civilizations of Asia. Perhaps even more disturbing was the growing popularity of pre-Christian paganism. Asia, having experienced the awesome destructive force of the new atomic age in the bombings of Hiroshima and Nagasaki, stood on the verge of revival. North America, having emerged from the

COMPARISON OF HISTORIC CHRISTIANITY, MODERNISM, AND NEO-ORTHODOXY

	Historic Christianity	Modernism (liberalism)	Neo-orthodoxy
Bible	Bible is Word of God	Purely human document recording humanity's quest for God	Human document that contains divine inspiration when read in faith
Salvation	Work of God's grace	Not necessary for individual, but reform of society is possible	Salvation as a religious experience of individual encountering God while reading Bible in faith; universal salvation implied
Assurance	Mixed. Some say yes; some say no	None	None
Church	Church in the body of Jesus Christ	Community of people for social reform	Prophetic community of "believers"

war unscathed and wallowing in material luxury, would experience an evangelical renaissance while itself becoming a mission field for Eastern mysticism and neo-paganism.

American evangelicalism after World War II followed three main lines of development. One was the continuation of fundamentalism, which became increasingly negative and anti-intellectual. Fundamentalism had served its purpose during the 1920s, heroically defending orthodox Christianity against theological liberalism. After World War II, however, fundamentalism no longer had a constructive role to play. Its extreme separatism and anti-intellectualism hindered the spread of the gospel by providing the opponents of Christianity with support for their charge that Christianity was no longer relevant to the modern world. Being inherently antiprogressive, fundamentalism seemed to defend an unjust socioeconomic system, while condemning all efforts at promoting justice in society as being somehow communist inspired. The defiant image of Alabama governor George C. Wallace, standing in the doorway to block admission of African-Americans to the University of Alabama, had its counterpart in the image of an equally defiant Jerry Falwell blocking admission of African-Americans to Thomas Road Baptist Church in Lynchburg, Virginia. It was a sad testimony of racism among Christians repeated throughout America, not solely in the South.

A second line of evangelical development was what might be called mainstream or "new-evangelicalism." The new-evangelicalism was characterized by its willingness to engage the postwar world through evangelism, scholarship, and (beginning in the 1980s) political and social action. Once again there was a unity of evangelism and social activism characteristic of true spiritual renewal. The new-evangelicalism was perhaps best exemplified in the ministries of its two most visible and effective representatives, Billy Graham and Francis A. Schaeffer.

William F. "Billy" Graham was born on a North Carolina farm in 1918 and converted to Christianity under the preaching of evangelist Mordecai Ham. After graduation from Wheaton College in 1943, Graham married Ruth Bell, daughter of Nelson Bell, a famous missionary to China. The first evangelist of Youth for Christ International (later known as Campus Life), Billy Graham's career as the most successful evangelist in modern church history took flight in 1949, when the Hearst newspaper chain reported on the phenomenal success of Graham's Los Angeles tent revival. Since the founding of the Billy Graham Evangelistic Association in 1950, the Billy Graham team has preached the gospel around the world. With access to the world's political leaders and a friendly relationship with the papacy, Graham became the leading spokesperson for evangelical Christianity. He was at the center of virtually every major event of evangelical Christianity during the second half of the century—from the founding of *Christianity Today* in 1956, to the Lausanne Congress on World Evangelism in 1974, and its follow-up meeting in Manila in 1989.

Billy Graham's personal integrity and the integrity of the Billy Graham Evangelistic Association—especially in financial matters—set an example that earned Graham and his team the respect and admiration of Christians and non-Christians alike. Outside of the condemnations of a few hard-core fundamentalists, it was hard to find anyone critical of Billy Graham. Unfortunately, the example he set was not always emulated by his contemporary televangelists and media stars—who provided the secular media with all too many scandals to report.

One of the keynote speakers at the Lausanne Congress was Francis A. Schaeffer (1912–1984), who came out of the fundamentalist ghetto to found L'Abri ministry in Switzerland. Francis and Edith Schaeffer went to Europe in 1948 as missionaries with the Independent Board for Presbyterian Foreign Missions. In 1955, they resigned from the mission board and began what later became known as L'Abri ("the Shelter"). During the 1960s and 1970s, L'Abri became a teaching center to which university students and professionals from all over the world would come. There, they studied the relevance of Christianity in a world rapidly slipping into postmodernity. A steady stream of books, and eventually a film series, flowed out of L'Abri, not only from the pen of Francis Schaeffer, but also from Edith Schaeffer and others who were either formally or informally a part of the L'Abri family.

Francis Schaeffer had an ability to communicate Christian truth and its relevance to modern culture in a way that the average educated layperson could understand. It may safely be said that no one since C. S. Lewis (1898–1963) did more to shape the thinking of evangelicals in the last half of the twentieth century. But it was not only as an apologist and evangelist to the modern intellectual that Schaeffer impacted evangelicalism. He also stirred the social conscience of evangelicals and galvanized them into action against racism and the increasing assault on the sanctity of human life. Prior to Schaeffer's clarion call to action (assisted by the noted physician, Dr. C. Everett Koop), the battles against abortion and euthanasia were left largely to Roman Catholics and Mormons. Evangelicals were passive, at best, preferring to emphasize personal salvation as the sole aspiration of the gospel. When Francis Schaeffer died in the summer of 1984, it was acceptable, even fashionable, for conservative evangelicals to be politically active—not only on sanctity of life issues, but on a whole host of social issues.[54]

A third line of development of postwar evangelicalism in America was its increasing bourgeoisification and penchant for civil religion. Americans after World War II were very serious about religion, but did not take religion very seriously. In other words, Americans flocked to the churches in unprecedented numbers, but largely as a vote of confidence in the American way of life. Traditional American values had triumphed over fascism and Japanese imperialism during the war, and Americans were confident that those values would triumph over atheistic communism in the Cold War. Middle-class Americans were affluent and proud. To be an American meant believing in God and opposing communism. This frame of mind was summed up in the phrases "In God We Trust" (which became the nation's official motto); "under God" (added to the Pledge of Allegiance in 1954); and in President Dwight Eisenhower's remark: "Our government makes no sense, unless it is founded in a deeply felt religious faith—and I don't care what it is."[55]

As affluence became a characteristic of mainstream evangelicalism, evangelicals fled the cities for the comfort and safety of the suburbs. As the cities began to change color (becoming the refuge of poor minorities), the white, middle-class, Protestant churches closed and moved out to the suburbs. There, evangelicals were able to insulate themselves from the harsh realities of an urban world in decay. This world was about to reap the pent-up whirlwind of rage arising from more than a century of social and economic injustice. During the 1950s, the two dominant val-

[54]One can only wonder what a difference it would have made for some evangelical leader like Francis Schaeffer to have been willing (as Wilberforce, Finney, or Shaftesbury would have been) to walk beside Martin Luther King Jr. in the Civil Rights struggle of the 1960s.
[55]Quoted in Marsden, *Religion and American Culture,* 214.

ues of Americans at large, including middle-class, suburban evangelicals, were what Francis A. Schaeffer characterized as personal peace ("not to be troubled by the troubles of other people, whether across the world or across the city") and affluence ("a life made up of things, things, and more things—a success judged by an ever-higher level of material abundance").[56]

The comfortable world of personal peace and affluence was shaken by the explosion of the 1960s. The Civil Rights movement was to finally bring a measure of social and economic justice to African-American and other ethnic minorities. Together with the resistance to what many Americans felt was a war of aggression against the people of Vietnam, it turned the streets and campuses of America into battlegrounds. The Civil Rights movement, and to a lesser extent the antiwar movement, was often led by liberal Christians. In the final analysis, the fact that the ideological revolt spread to Europe and even Japan was evidence that it was a revolt against the two horrendous values of personal peace and affluence and was a search for new values.

Once again, conservative evangelicals allied themselves with those who defended the status quo. The spectacle of conservative pastors defending segregation as somehow biblical had its counterpart in the spectacle of the new evangelical media stars, like Jerry Falwell, touring the nation holding "I Love America" rallies. Such Christians correctly sensed that a paradigm shift was taking place in American values. The traditional values of a white, Protestant, Anglo-Saxon America, still dominant during the 1950s, was yielding the field to a pluralism of values associated with a multicultural society.

By the 1990s, evangelical Christians were largely purged from the mainstream of American life. They were relegated to the fringe of public life, where they no longer influenced American culture. Only in politics, where conservative politicians courted the so-called "Religious Right" as a dependable voting block (a

[56]Francis A. Schaeffer, *How Should We Then Live? The Rise and Decline of Western Thought and Culture* (Old Tappan, NJ: Fleming H. Revell Co., 1976), 205.

revival of the old "Republican party at prayer"), did they exert any influence. Even in politics, however, their influence was largely limited to keeping economic conservatives in power. The conservative politicians gave little in return for their support. The secularization of American society went on unabated. Evangelicals were too often preoccupied with the myth of a Christian America. As before in their history, they expended their energies fighting a battle that was irrelevant to the outcome of the real war—the culture war—that Christians were losing almost without a struggle.

It was not, however, all gloom and doom for evangelicals. Evangelicalism was revived, and some might add redeemed, by movements outside the churches that arose from the troubled 1960s and 1970s. Out of the 1960s counterculture of San Francisco's Haight-Ashbury came the "Jesus People." Adopting the appearance of the counterculture, these enthusiasts stressed Bible study and aggressive witnessing on the streets and in coffee houses. Campus Crusade for Christ International, founded by Bill Bright, had thirteen thousand full-time staff members organizing personal evangelism ministries on university campuses in 1994. Campus Life, Young Life, Navigators, and InterVarsity Christian Fellowship likewise met the youth of the post-1960s revolution on their own turf. Those who normally would not enter a church or go to a crusade were confronted with the claims of Jesus Christ by Christians of their own generation, who spoke their language.

By the late 1970s, evangelicals were recapturing a vision for spiritual renewal, combining evangelism with social reform. More than fifty evangelical leaders met over Thanksgiving weekend in 1973 and issued the Declaration of Social Concern. This declaration expressed repentance for past failures and called for efforts to achieve a just society. Ron Sider's *Rich Christians in an Age of Hunger: A Biblical Study* (1977) called upon evangelicals to reassess their affluence in light of the poverty that engulfed much of the world's population. Parachurch ministries like World Vision International and Samaritan's Purse tried to meet the challenge. By the last decade of the century, Southern Baptists were officially repenting and asking forgiveness for their past racism, which they correctly called sin. Even in Mississippi, white and African-American Christians came together in interracial, nondenominational ministries like Voice of Calvary and Mission Mississippi to demonstrate that racial reconciliation was possible through the power of the Holy Spirit.

At the close of the century there were reasons for both rejoicing and concern. Christianity as a whole was growing at a rate of 2.9 percent—approximately twice that of the world's population (1.7 percent). Much of this growth was in Latin America, Africa, and the East Asian Pacific Rim.[57] There, the growth was among the evangelical churches. The mainline churches—those that were influenced by liberal theologies—suffered decline worldwide, both in membership and their involvement in world missions. In Europe and North America, growth among the evangelical churches was mainly by transfer from liberal churches and by birth. Roman Catholicism grew at a slower rate, despite the reforms of the Vatican II Council and the immense popularity of Pope John-Paul II. The Roman Catholic church lost many members to secularism in Europe and North America (as did the Protestants), and to evangelicalism in Latin America.

In Africa, where Christian missionaries were introduced in large numbers only with the beginning of the age of imperialism (c. 1875 to 1900), the Christian faith made great strides, despite instability and persecution. Following the end of imperialism, the decade of the 1960s saw the greatest growth. By 1980, over one-half of the continent's population, approximately 275 million people, was Christian. Of these, only about twenty-six million were evangelicals.

The 1970s saw spectacular growth in Latin America, nominally Roman Catholic for over five hundred years. Between 1900 and 1990, the number of evangelical Christians rose from two

[57] Statistics in this section are from Patrick Johnstone, *The Church Is Bigger Than You Think* (Fearn, Ross-shire, UK: Christian Focus Publications, 1998), 109-116 and Cairns *Christianity Through the Centuries,* 507, 522-524.

hundred fifty thousand to forty million. In the year 2000, the number was thought to be as high as sixty million. There are now more evangelicals in Brazil than in the whole of Europe.

The 1980s and 1990s have witnessed spectacular church growth in the Asian nations, where there are more evangelicals today than in North America. In Seoul, Korea, where just over a century ago there was not a single evangelical congregation, there are today seven of the ten largest evangelical churches in the world. At least eleven million people, approximately 25 percent of the Korean population, are Protestants—mostly evangelical. In China, the number of Protestants grew from approximately one million in 1949 (the year the communists came to power), to more than fifty million in 1990. Evidence of the spiritual life of these churches can be seen in their commitment to missions. The Korean churches send out approximately twenty-five hundred missionaries, while the churches of Singapore send out more missionaries per capita than any other churches in the world.

The phenomenal growth of Christianity outside the West is all the more remarkable in light of the fact that it has often occurred in the face of increasing persecution. More Christians have died for their faith in the twentieth century than in the whole previous history of the church. According to the United States State Department, Christians face persecution in more than sixty countries around the world. In the Islamic state of Sudan, more than one million Christians have died for their faith. Many have been sold into slavery or physically mutilated. An average of one hundred and fifty thousand Christians are martyred every year. Vietnam, Indonesia, Sudan, China, Colombia, and India are only a partial list of countries where Christians suffered martyrdom at the end of the twentieth century.

Over the past two thousand years, the flame has burned brightly at times—while at other times and in certain places it has grown dim, or even been extinguished. Still, the church marches on triumphant, for it is not dependent upon the will of human beings, but rather upon the work of the Holy Spirit. To the church, the body of Christ, the Lord has given the keys, "and the gates of Hades will not overcome it" (Matthew 16:18).

TIMELINE FOR CHAPTER 10

1909	*Scofield Reference Bible* is published
1910–1915	*The Fundamentals* are published
1914–1918	World War I
1917	The Russian Revolution
1919	Eighteenth Amendment establishes prohibition in America
	Karl Barth's *Commentary on Romans* is published
1923	J. Gresham Machen's *Christianity and Liberalism* is published
1924	Johnson-Reed Act is passed by Congress, limiting immigration
1925	Scopes Trial in Dayton, Tennessee
1933	Hitler comes to power, signing *Reichkonkordat* with the Catholic Church
1934	The Confessing Church is organized and issues Barmen Declaration
1937	Pius XI issues *Divini Redemptoris* and *Mit brennender Sorge*
1939–1945	World War II
1949	Billy Graham's Los Angeles Crusade
1950	Billy Graham Evangelistic Association founded
1951	Campus Crusade for Christ International founded
1955	Francis A. and Edith Schaeffer found L'Abri Fellowship
1961	Berlin Wall erected
1962–1965	Vatican II Council
1974	Lausanne Congress on world evangelism
	Vietnam War ends
1978	John-Paul II elected
1989	Lausanne II Congress in Manila
	Fall of the Berlin Wall
1991	End of the Soviet Union

THE CHURCH IN A NEW MILLENNIUM
. . . .

If the individual living at the dawn of the twenty-first century could be transported back one hundred years to the beginning of the twentieth century, the thing that would most likely impress him or her would be the domination of the world by Western civilization. Before World War I, most of the world was ruled by Western nations. So closely linked were Christianity and Western civilization over the previous sixteen hundred years, that many Christians equated the Westernization of the world with its Christianization. Now, one hundred years later, with the decline of Western domination everywhere, many Christians are confused. They misinterpret the passing of Western cultural dominance and the emergence of a multicultural world civilization as Christianity in crisis—perhaps its very existence threatened.

The crisis in Christendom has led many Christians to adopt a siege mentality. Rather than asserting their spiritual authority and going on the offensive in evangelizing the world, they are engaged in a fruitless attempt to save Christendom. In America, this often takes the form of efforts to recapture some past golden age, when America was allegedly a Christian nation. Just as Americans at the turn of the century felt threatened by immigrants from eastern and western Europe, many evangelical Christians today feel threatened by multiculturalism.

Christianity, having developed within Western civilization, has become encumbered with a lot of Western cultural baggage. In chapter 1, we noted that the task given by the Lord to his followers was to proclaim the Good News (gospel) of salvation by grace through faith in the risen Lord Jesus Christ to all who would hear and believe. We also noted that from the very beginning, the institutional church has been influenced by the culture in which it has existed. How we worship, how we baptize or celebrate the Lord's Supper, even how we construct our church buildings are all culturally influenced. Does it really matter whether we worship in a sanctuary or out in the open air? Does it really matter whether we celebrate Communion with grape juice (or wine) and wafers, or berry juice and sweet potatoes as do some Christians in Irian Jaya?

The passing of Western cultural dominance, far from being a threat to the existence of Christianity, offers the opportunity for the church to shed its cultural baggage and become once again what it was during the first three centuries: a pilgrim church. We should welcome the end of an era of the imperial church that has dominated since the time of Constantine. By separating from the culture and letting go of the reins of power, Christians may once again regain their prophetic voice. As Douglas John Hall has suggested, the church may once again become "salt, yeast, and light" in the world.[58] The pilgrim church of the next century will be one that no longer enjoys the protection and favor of the state. It will once again face persecution, but having been refined by fire, will once again turn the world upside down, just as it did with the Roman Empire. This will not occur by human power, but by the power of the Holy Spirit.

We must not mourn the end of Christendom, as though Christendom and the Christian church were one and the same thing. This is the mistake made by those who seek the world's salva-

---

[58] *The End of Christendom and the Future of Christianity* (Valley Forge, PA: Trinity Press International, 1997) cited in Patrick Johnstone, *The Church Is Bigger Than You Think*, 262.

tion through the mobilization of political influence by some sort of "moral majority" or "religious right." We must realize, as Patrick Johnstone points out, that "the coming of Christianity did not convert [the West] but 'baptized' the paganism that still has to be adequately confronted with the claims of Christ."[59] The neo-pagan world of the twenty-first century needs the witness of a spiritually revived Christianity that once again—as in its first centuries—is "unafraid to love and win those who persecute it."[60]

ABOUT THE AUTHOR
. . . .

Paul R. Waibel is professor of history at Belhaven College. He is the author of *Politics of Accommodation* (1983), coauthor (with Michael D. Richards) of *Twentieth-Century Europe: A Brief History* (1999), and has published numerous articles and reviews in scholarly journals, periodicals, reference works, and anthologies. Professor Waibel holds degrees in history from Lynchburg College, Virginia Tech, and West Virginia University. He was a Fulbright-Hayes Scholar at the Univesity of Bonn, Germany, and an NEH Fellow at the University of California, Berkeley.

[59] Johnstone, *The Church Is Bigger Than You Think*, 263.
[60] Ibid.

BIBLIOGRAPHY

The following is a select list of suggested books for the reader who wishes additional reading on limited topics. The list is meant to be brief, approximately five titles per chapter, and includes both scholarly studies, as well as those of a more popular nature. The bibliographies of these might in turn be consulted for further suggestions.

GENERAL HISTORIES AND REFERENCE WORKS

Askew, Thomas A. and Peter W. Spellman. *The Churches and the American Experience: Ideals and Institutions.* Grand Rapids, MI: Baker Book House, 1984. A very readable survey of American church history.

Cairns, Earle E. *Christianity Through the Centuries: A History of the Christian Church.* 3rd. ed. Grand Rapids, MI: Zondervan Publishing Co., 1996. The classic one-volume survey textbook on church history, translated into many languages.

Bainton, Roland H. *Christendom: A Short History of Christianity and Its Impact on Western Civilization.* 2 vols. New York: Harper Torchbooks, 1966. A well-written survey by a leading church historian and authority on the Reformation.

Clouse, Robert G., Richard V. Pierard, and Edwin M. Yamauchi. *Two Kingdoms: The Church and Culture Through the Ages.* Chicago: Moody Press, 1993. A survey of church history and its interaction with secular culture.

Douglas, J. D., gen. ed. *The New International Dictionary of the Christian Church.* Grand Rapids, MI: Zondervan Publishing House, 1978. A basic alphabetical guide to who's who, and what's what in church history.

Dowley, Tim, org. ed. *Eerdmans' Handbook to the History of Christianity.* Grand Rapids, MI: Wm. B. Eerdmans Publishing Co., 1977. A good chronological and thematic guide to church history.

Jackson, Jeremy C. *No Other Foundation: The Church Through Twenty Centuries.* Westchester, IL: Cornerstone Books, 1980. An interesting and provocative interpretation of church history by the chief historical researcher for the film series *How Should We Then Live?*

Latourette, Kenneth Scott. *A History of Christianity.* New York: Harper & Row, 1953. A detailed history of the church by one of the century's leading church historians.

Marsden, George M. *Religion and American Culture.* New York: Harcourt Brace Jovanovich, Publishers, 1990. A very informative survey of American church history and the role of religion in shaping American culture, while being shaped by it.

Noll, Mark A., *et. al.,* eds. *Eerdmans' Handbook to Christianity in America.* Grand Rapids, MI: William B. Eerdmans Publishing Co., 1983. A chronological and topical survey of major themes in American church history.

—. *Turning Points: Decisive Moments in the History of Christianity.* Grand Rapids, MI: Baker Book House, 1997. A very readable and informative look at twelve key events in church history (e.g., Council of Nicaea, Diet of Worms, etc.).

Schaeffer, Francis A. *How Should We Then Live? The Rise and Decline of Western Thought and Culture.* Old Tappan, NJ: Fleming Revell Co., 1976. Popular interpretation of the history of Western society from a Christian perspective.

Schaff, Philip. *History of the Christian Church.* 3rd ed. 8 vols. Lanham, MD: Hendrickson Publishers, 1996. A classic history of the church through the Reformation, originally published in 1910.

Shelley, Bruce L. *Church History in Plain Language.* Waco, TX: Word Books, 1982. A basic one-volume survey of church history.

CHAPTERS 1–3

Bredero, Adrian H. *Christendom and Christianity in the Middle Ages: The Relations between Religion, Church, and Society.* Grand Rapids, MI: Wm. B. Eerdmans Publishing Co., 1986. Addresses the issue of how the medieval church was molded by medieval society.

Cahill, Thomas. *How the Irish Saved Civilization: The Untold Story of Ireland's Heroic Role from the Fall of Rome to the Rise of Medieval Europe.* New York: Doubleday, 1995. A look at how the monks of the Irish Celtic church saved civilization by preserving books.

Chadwick, Henry. *The Early Church.* Grand Rapids, MI: Wm. B. Eerdmans Publishing Co., 1967. Relates the church's history to the social and ideological context in which it emerged.

Davis, Leo Donald. *The First Seven Ecumenical Councils, 325-787: Their History and Theology.* Wilmington, DE: Michael Glazier, Inc., 1987. A Jesuit scholar looks at the key ecumenical councils that defined orthodoxy.

Dawson, Christopher. *The Formation of Christendom.* New York: Sheed and Ward, Inc., 1967. The rise of the medieval world and how it was shaped by the church.

Frend, W. H. C. *The Rise of Christianity.* Philadelphia: Fortress Press, 1984. A massive detailed survey of the infant church from its Jewish background to the end of the sixth century.

Green, Julien. *God's Fool: The Life and Times of Francis of Assisi.* San Francisco: Harper & Row, 1985. A very readable and interesting biography of St. Francis and the world he lived in.

Hillgarth, J. N., ed. *Christianity and Paganism, 350-750: The Conversion of Western Europe.* Philadelphia: University of Pennsylvania Press, 1986. The struggle to convert and civilize the Germanic tribes, especially in the former western Roman Empire.

Maier, Paul L. *In the Fullness of Time: A Historian Looks at Christmas, Easter, and the Early Church.* San Francisco: HarperSanFrancisco, 1991. Three classic volumes under one cover that bring to life the history and archeology of the New Testament.

Mattingly, Harold. *Christianity in the Roman Empire.* New York: W. W. Norton & Co., 1967. A clear, well-written introduction to the relations of church and state in the Roman Empire.

Payne, Robert. *The Making of the Christian World From Christ to Dante.* New York: Dorset Press, 1966. Well-written, vivid account of the formation of the church during the early centuries.

Peters, Edward, ed. *Monks, Bishops and Pagans: Christian Culture in Gaul and Italy, 500-700.* Philadelphia: University of Pennsylvania Press, 1975. Modern translations of works by Gregory the Great, Bede, St. Benedict, and Gregory of Tours.

Smith, M. A. *From Christ to Constantine.* Downers Grove, IL: InterVarsity Press, 1971. Short survey of the church in the Roman Empire to its legalization under Constantine. It covers various aspects of church life—baptism, Lord's Supper, hymns, discipline, etc.— during the period of the New Testament.

Southern, R. W. *Western Society and the Church in the Middle Ages.* Grand Rapids, MI: Wm. B. Eerdmans Publishing Co., 1970. A survey of medieval church history from c. 700 to c. 1520.

Wagner, Walter H. *After the Apostles: Christianity in the Second Century.* Minneapolis: Fortress Press, 1994. The main events, movements, and people during the period when Christianity was separating from Judaism.

Workman, Herbert B. *Persecution in the Early Church.* New York: Oxford University Press, 1980. A vivid portrayal of the sufferings of the martyrs of the first Christian centuries.

CHAPTERS 4–6

Bainton, Roland H. *Here I Stand: A Life of Martin Luther.* Nashville: Abingdon Press, 1978. First published in 1950, this classic remains the best biography of Martin Luther.

—. *The Reformation of the Sixteenth Century.* London: Hodder and Stoughton, 1963. A good one-volume history of the Reformation by the dean of Reformation historians.

—. *Women of the Reformation: From Spain to Scandinavia.* Minneapolis: Augsburg Publishing House, 1977. A look at the contributions of the many female heroes of the Reformation.

Bouwsma, William J. *John Calvin: A Sixteenth Century Portrait.* New York: Oxford University Press, 1989. The life and times of the Geneva reformer and founder of the Reformed faith.

Burckhardt, Jacob. *The Civilization of the Renaissance in Italy.* 2 vols. New York: Harper Colophon Books, 1958. An illustrated and very enjoyable history of the Renaissance by the German-Swiss historian who defined the Renaissance as a distinct period, when he first published this study in the 1860s.

Butterfield, Herbert. *The Origins of Modern Science.* New York: Macmillan, 1962. A classic, provocative, and informative history of the Scientific Revolution from the Middle Ages through the Enlightenment.

Dillenberger, John. *Martin Luther: Selections from his Writings.* New York: Doubleday & Co., 1961. Shows the development of Luther's thought through selections from his writings.

Edwards, Brian H. *God's Outlaw: The Story of William Tyndale and the English Bible.* Welwyn, Herts.: Evangelical Press, 1982. Very readable and heroic tale of the man who put the Bible into English.

Estep, William R. *Renaissance and Reformation.* Grand Rapids, MI: William B.

Eerdmans Publishing Co., 1986. A survey of church history during the Renaissance and Reformation with emphasis on the Reformation and the Anabaptists.

Goertz, Hans-Jurgen, ed. *Profiles of Radical Reformers*. Scottdale, PA: Herald Press, 1982. Brief biographical sketches of the leaders of the Radical Reformation.

Hillerbrand, Hans J. *Men and Ideas in the Sixteenth Century*. Prospect Heights, IL: Waveland Press, Inc., 1969. An interesting brief synthesis of facts and interpretation that tries to understand the Reformation and its relationship to European society in the sixteenth century.

—. *The Reformation: A Narrative History Related by Contemporary Observers and Participants*. Grand Rapids, MI: Baker Book House, 1982. A history of the Reformation as told through the documents.

Hummel, Charles E. *The Galileo Connection: Resolving Conflicts between Science & the Bible*. Downers Grove, IL: InterVarsity Press, 1986. Puts the conflict between the Bible and science in historical context by telling the stories of Copernicus, Kepler, Galileo, and Newton.

Jones, R. Tudur. *The Great Reformation: A Wide-Ranging Survey of the Beginnings of Protestantism*. Downers Grove, IL: InterVarsity Press, 1985. A basic history that covers the major events in the Reformation in Germany, Switzerland, England, France, and Italy, as well as the Protestant impulse from Finland to Wales, from Hungary to Spain.

Klassen, Peter J. *European in the Reformation*. Englewood Cliffs, NJ: Prentice-Hall, Inc., 1979. A good basic history of the Reformation.

Noll, Mark A. ed. *Confessions and Catechisms of the Reformation*. Grand Rapids, MI: Baker Book House, 1991. English translations of the great confessional documents of the Reformation from Luther's Ninety-five Theses to the Thirty-nine Articles of the Church of England.

Oakley, Francis. *The Western Church in the Later Middle Ages*. Ithaca, NY: Cornell University Press, 1979. A look at the fourteenth and fifteenth centuries and the movements—e.g., *devotio moderna*, popular piety, Great Schism—that led to the Protestant Reformation.

Parker, T. H. L. *Calvin: An Introduction to His Thought*. Lanham, MD: Westminster John Knox, 1995. A look at the ideas of the second most important figure in the Protestant Reformation.

Potter, G. R. *Zwingli*. New York: Cambridge University Press, 1984. A scholarly look at the life of the Great Swiss Reformer.

Roper, William. *The Life of Sir Thomas More*. Springfield, IL: Templegate Publishers, n.d. A reprint of the biography of Thomas More by his son-in-law.

Wilcox, Donald J. *In Search of God & Self: Renaissance and Reformation Thought*. Prospect Heights, IL: Waveland Press, Inc., 1987. Emphasizes the intellectual and cultural history of the Renaissance and Reformation.

CHAPTERS 8–10

Altyholz, Josef L. *The Churches in the Nineteenth Century*. Indianapolis: Bobbs-Merrill, 1967. A survey of church history during the age of the secularization of culture.

Battiscombe, Georgiana. *Shaftesbury: A Biography of the Seventh Earl, 1801-1885*. Boston: Houghton Mifflin, 1975. A balanced and well-documented biography of the great evangelical reformer.

Brown, Dale W. *Understanding Pietism*. Lanham, MD: Evangelical Publishing House, 1996. A classic attempt to access and define pietism by seeing it in its historical context.

Cragg, Gerald. *The Church and the Age of Reason, 1648-1789*. Grand Rapids, MI:

William B. Eerdmans Publishing Co., 1962. A survey of church history during the era when Western civilization made the break with its Christian past and embraced a secular worldview.

Dayton, Donald W. *Discovering an Evangelical Heritage.* San Francisco: Harper & Row, 1976. Demonstrates that the leaders of abolitionism, feminism, and social welfare movements in nineteenth-century America came from the ranks of the evangelicals.

Dorsett, Lyle W. *A Passion for Souls: The Life of D. L. Moody.* Chicago: Moody Press, 1997. A well-written biography that captures the meaning of Moody's life and ministry.

Drummond, Lewis A. *Spurgeon: Prince of the Preachers.* Lanham, MD: Kregel, 1992. The life of Britain's equivalent of D. L. Moody.

Edwards, Brian H. *Through Many Dangers: The Story of John Newton.* Lanham, MD: Evangelical Press, 1994. The amazing story of the author of "Amazing Grace."

Hardman, Keith J. *Charles Grandison Finney, 1772-1875.* Syracuse: Syracuse University Press, 1988. Covers the full sweep of Finney's life and work as theologian, revivalist, and educator.

Howse, Ernest. *Saints in Politics.* Toronto: Toronto University Press, 1952. The lives and works of members of the Clapham Sect.

Lovelace, Richard F. *Dynamics of Spiritual Life: An Evangelical Theology of Renewal.* Exeter, Eng.: The Paternoster Press, 1979. An excellent history of the relationship between spiritual renewal and social reform.

Murray, Iain H. *Jonathan Edwards: A New Biography.* Lanham, MD: Banner of Truth, 1987. A good, thorough biography of one of America's greatest intellects.

Olland, S. L. *A Short History of the Oxford Movement.* London: Mowbray, 1983.

Orr, J. Edwin. *The Light of Nations.* Grand Rapids, MI: William B. Eerdmans Publishing Co., 1965. A leading church historian looks at the history of revivals and their impact between 1789 and 1860.

Tucker, Ruth A. *From Jerusalem to Irian Jaya: A Biographical History of Christian Missions.* Grand Rapids, MI: Academic Books, 1983. A history of foreign missions as seen through short biographical sketches of famous missionaries.

Weinlick, John R. *Count Zinzendorf.* Nashville: Abingdon Press, 1961. A popular biography, illustrated and well written.

Wood, A. Skevington. *The Burning Light.* Grand Rapids, MI: William B. Eerdmans Publishing Co., 1967. A well-researched and balanced account of John Wesley's life and work.

CHAPTER 10

Catherwood, Christopher. *Five Evangelical Leaders.* Wheaton, IL: Harold Shaw Publishers, 1985. Short biographies of five of the most influential evangelicals of the century: John Stott, Martyn Lloyd-Jones, Francis Schaeffer, J. I. Packer, and Billy Graham.

Detzler, Wayne A. *The Changing Church in Europe.* Grand Rapids, MI: Zondervan, 1979. Looks at the state of religion in contemporary Europe.

Dorsett, Lyle W. *Billy Sunday and the Redemption of Urban America.* Grand Rapids, MI: William B. Eerdmans Publishing Co., 1991. Using the Sunday family papers, Dorsett presents a new look at the greatest tabernacle revivalist.

Fowler, Robert Booth. *A New Engagement: Evangelical Political Thought, 1966-1976.* Grand Rapids, MI: William B. Eerdmans Publishing Co., 1982. A survey of the diverse evangelical political and social attitudes during the formative decade between the Vietnam War and the Carter presidency.

Guinness, Os. *Dining with the Devil*. Grand Rapids, MI: Baker Book House, 1993. A critique of the rise of the megachurch.

—. *Fit Bodies: Fat Minds*. Grand Rapids, MI: Baker Book House, 1995. Recounts the failure of both liberal and evangelical Christians to confront modern culture with biblical truth.

Graham, Billy. *Just As I Am: The Autobiography of Billy Graham*. San Francisco: Harper & Row, 1997. A personal look at the life of the century's most respected Christian leader.

Horton, Michael Scott. *Made in America: The Shaping of Modern American Evangelicalism*. Grand Rapids, MI: Baker Book House, 1991. An unflattering look at how much of contemporary American evangelicalism is characterized by a subjective pursuit of the trivial.

Johnstone, Patrick. *The Church is Bigger Than You Think: The Unfinished Work of World Evangelisation*. Fearn, Ross-shire, UK: Christian Focus Publications, 1998. An excellent source on the state of the faith at the end of the twentieth century and its prospects for the next century.

Linder, Robert D. and Richard V. Pierard. *Twilight of the Saints: Biblical Christianity & Civil Religion in America*. Downers Grove, IL: InterVarsity Press, 1978. An attempt to define civil religion by looking at its history in America.

Marsden, George M. *Fundamentalism and American Culture: The Shaping of Twentieth-Century Evangelicalism, 1870-1925*. New York: Oxford University Press, 1980. The classic interpretive history of fundamentalism in America.

Parkhurst, Jr., Louis Gifford. *Francis Schaeffer: The Man and His Message*. Wheaton, IL: Tyndale House Publishers, Inc., 1985. A personal look at the life and work of Schaeffer by a friend.

Schultze, Quentin J. *Televangelism and American Culture: The Business of Popular Religion*. Grand Rapids, MI: Baker Book House, 1991. A look at how televangelists destroy their ministries by trading entertaining images for solid teaching.

Taylor, Kenneth N. *My Life: A Guided Tour*. Wheaton, IL: Tyndale House Publishers, Inc., 1991. The autobiography of the man who prepared the most readable of all English Bible versions.

INDEX